TO BE A SAUDI

To my dearest Julia,
Just a few words and a ton of dreams,
With my warmest wishes and respect.

H— Y——

TO BE A SAUDI

HANI A. Z. YAMANI

JANUS PUBLISHING COMPANY
London, England

First published in Great Britain 1997
by Janus Publishing Company Limited,
Edinburgh House, 19 Nassau Street,
London W1N 7RE

Re-printed 1998

www.januspublishing.co.uk

A CIP catalogue record for this book
is available from the British Library.

ISBN 1 85756 303 4

Phototypeset in 11 on 12³/₁ Baskerville
by Keyboard Services, Lutton, Beds

Printed and bound in Great Britain by
Antony Rowe Ltd, Chippenham, Wiltshire

This book is dedicated to my children Laila, Ayah, and Ahmad, and all their young brothers and sisters in Saudi Arabia.

Contents

Prologue

THE LAST few years have marked our dependence on the information highway. As a businessman who travels over 200,000 miles a year, I depend on the news in many of my investment assessments. I take the information which millions of humans are sharing and by using what I hope is intelligence and experience, I try to gain an edge over other investors. If God, or fate as the non-believers will call it, is willing, I will be successful in my business life.

With my reliance on the information highway is the knowledge, from past personal experience, that the news can sometimes be based on distorted reality. This can be because of poor communications, or because the person processing that news has his own views and agenda. Regardless of the reasons, this world which we now call the global village sometimes co-exists in flawed terms of understanding.

While I am travelling, I am on a constant search for news on Saudi Arabia. It is my country, where I was born and bred, and all my family live there. It is not enough just to telephone home, I find a need to read about any news related to the land where I belong. With this natural preoccupation has come a growing frustration and genuine worry with the type of news I read on Saudi Arabia in some of the international press. One day we are on the verge of national bankruptcy, the next we are preparing for civil war. If you compare this to the news you hear when inside the country, you would probably think that you are on a different planet, with different perceptions of reality. This situation has started me thinking: what is the real Saudi Arabia? Where do we stand as a nation? How do we compare with other nations in the world? What is going to be the future for our children? Is what we read sometimes about a growing internal malaise the truth?

So I started to study things carefully, looking into our past and present in their factual form, hoping to understand in this way more clearly our situation and our future. What I have discovered each passing day is a different Saudi Arabia than the one I thought I knew. I realised where we were 50 years ago, where we are at present, and I started dreaming of where our children will be in the twenty-first century. It is my discovery which I wanted to share with my fellow Saudis, as well as those foreigners who may wish to view Saudi Arabia through inquisitive native eyes. Before foreigners can hope to understand us, we must first understand ourselves what it means to be Saudis, and we must then fully communicate this vision of our realities to outsiders.

It was always an enigma for me to comprehend the true depth of the interest which the world has for Saudi Arabia, and which is translated by the confusing manner in which we are sometimes viewed as a people. The realities of my nation and my fellow Saudis, and the position that Saudi Arabia now holds in the 'New World Order', have made my understanding of certain foreign attitudes towards us much clearer. The motives and views of the foreign press represent the feelings of foreign interests towards my country, and this is in turn demonstrative of the importance that we Saudis are given.

Clarifying our realities is therefore of crucial importance for us, as well as for all those who are affected by our very existence on this planet. The need to know the truth about Saudi Arabia is further compounded by the international effects of all events and developments in the country, in addition to their direct influence on our daily lives as Saudis.

If you believe that you have discovered the truth, then it is natural that you will find it important to share it with others. To share a discovery means writing a book, which is something that none of my friends would encourage me to do. Writing a book with the topic that I want means exposure to public attention, discussions of controversial subjects, and antagonising some of those who do not agree with my assessments. Contrary to nations such as France and the US, amongst many others, where matters of all levels of importance are discussed openly and debated in the media, we Saudis are much more introverted, with a clear preference for private discussions between us than for writing books that try to communicate our true realities to all those who care to know. But not writing is, in my personal view, neglecting the country I love and being disloyal to my children. So, I write on Saudi Arabia regardless of the immediate reactions, may these words contribute in a small way to better comprehension and improved future prosperity. I hope that the result of my writing will be a positive example of objective and respectful analysis for other Saudis to follow and improve upon.

This book is not intended as an academic source for future generations, but it tries to achieve self-realisation of clear facts, and views these in a logical, regional and international context. In this analysis, I have tried to be objective, balanced, and honest. I must say that it is not easy to analyse your country in such an impartial manner, as there are always emotions of nationalism permeating every idea and discussion. All I can state is that I have sincerely attempted to let logic and facts override any personal emotions in my discussion of the realities of the present situation in my country, and I have freed my own feelings for my proposed solutions and future strategies. These are my personal suggestions, based on my own research and assessments, which the readers should evaluate in their proper context.

Let us then start on our journey of discovery by looking at the three characteristics that have shaped present-day Saudi Arabia and that will certainly influence its future to a great extent.

Part One

Why We Are

1

The Land of Islam

IF ANY single factor has shaped the history and character of Saudi Arabia, it is certainly Islam. From the day Al Wahee (the revelation) came to prophet Muhammad, peace be upon him, over 14 centuries ago, the destiny of this land became an integral part of the Muslim religion. The two holiest cities in Islam, Makkah and Madinah, are in Saudi Arabia, making the country the focal point for over one billion Muslims worldwide. This is surely a blessing of immense magnitude for the people of Saudi Arabia, but it can also represent a significant pressure on the country if this honour is not handled correctly.

Islam is totally ingrained in the fabric of contemporary Saudi life and this is perhaps beyond the comprehension of many foreigners. All Saudis are Muslims, with a vast majority of them as true believers and practitioners. Sharia (Islamic doctrine) is the law and constitution of the land. The Sunna (the tradition of the Prophet) regulates daily life. Al-Shahada (the Oath to God) forms the Saudi Arabian flag. The King is the Custodian of The Two Holy Mosques. No other country on earth is so regulated and influenced at all levels by any religion like Saudi Arabia is by Islam.

As the Kingdom has embarked on a major modernisation programme over the last few decades, fuelled by the developments in the oil industry, Islam has in no way diminished in its supreme importance to the country and its people. As contemporary tools are injected in the daily activities of the population, this has always been implemented in complete adherence with Islamic doctrine, and in a progressive manner that does not disturb Muslim values.

The continued importance of the Muslim religion in Saudi Arabian life and development is basically due to the very nature of Islam. It proves daily that it is very complete, and adaptable to every time, without any changes to the basics being required or accepted. It is a constitution, a law, an economic path, a social regulator, and God's eternal instructions. As such, it has proven itself in the eyes of the believers as the only reliable and divine way of life, offering humans the preferred path for all conditions and times.

To the outsider, Islam marks daily life in Saudi Arabia in visual modes: prayers five times each day, the fast in Ramadan, the pilgrimage season, the veil for women, etc ... Real effects of Islam on Saudi society are much more important and profound. It shapes our family relations, our education system, our social fabric, our future aspirations, and the manner in which we view life itself. We are what we are because we are first and foremost Muslims. Islam brought us out of the darkness and taught us love and respect. Islam gave us the knowledge which we spread throughout the world. Islam ingrained in us hope and dignity – may our children's tomorrow be better than our forefathers' yesterday.

Islam will continue to play a vital role in the lives of the people of Saudi Arabia and it will prevail in the future as the greatest influence in the country. Some will call this continued conservatism, even fundamentalism, but I prefer to say it is pure enlightenment. It is certainly an enormous stabilising factor with great benefits to the ideology and social adherence of the population. It has had crucial positive effects during the frantic development in the past 50 years when change could have led to strong confusion in Saudi life, as it has done in certain other Third World countries with even more regular rates of economic growth (i.e., Algeria, Iran, Nigeria, etc.). Islam will continue to hold together the fabric of Saudi society in the twenty-first century and beyond.

We will see in later chapters the effects of the application of Islam on the economy and society of present-day Saudi Arabia, and whether any modifications should be made on certain applied practices in the country to increase efficiency and avoid future problems. It is clear that any modifications of presently applied practices must take into account the true feelings of the people of the country, who are in majority more conservative than many analysts seem to realise, and who do not wish to see any deviation from recognised Islamic doctrine. It is therefore clear that any future reform in Saudi Arabia must demonstrate its adherence to the Sharia (Islamic Law) and the Sunna (the tradition of the Prophet), and be of necessity for the entire nation rather than just a preference for a minority of Saudis. The full adherence of reforms to Islam should never be only in name, but in our soul and spirit, as life must always represent true beliefs and not mere wishes.

We should also avoid modifying the clear parameters of our religion, in a manner that changes God's intent, to comfort our own fears and complexes. Such a blunder may thwart our development, promote extremism in our society, and misrepresent the beautiful characteristics that make Islam the eternal path for happiness and salvation.

2

The Power of Oil

THE Saudi Arabian sands have beneath them 25 per cent of the recognised world oil reserves. In other words, the world is economically dependent on the Kingdom. It is true that the citizens of this planet are interdependent, but this is at varying degrees. Pollution in one country affects others. A banking crisis in one nation can have serious global repercussions. But a durable shut-down in the Saudi oil-fields would have devastating effects on the world economy beyond what can ever be imagined. Western economies would go into a deep depression for several years. Oil prices would attain rates beyond the reach of most nations and every facet of our daily life would be changed in a dramatic manner. There is no alternative to Saudi oil supply at present and this situation will continue as long as hydro-carbons are the main global source of energy.

The advent of oil on the Saudi scene has been of primary importance to the country in this century. From a poor nation of Bedouins, fragmented into scattered tribes, and whose only source of foreign income came from pilgrims to the holy cities, Saudi Arabia is today a rich and modern nation, with all the amenities of wealth and affluence. In the club of powerful nations, Saudi Arabia is a player of great importance. Had an astrologer predicted this development at the beginning of the century, he would have been labelled a crazy fool. Yet it is today a reality which the world must live with, and which we as Saudis must fully comprehend and assume as a serious responsibility. The power of oil is immense, thanks to the income it generates, but much more because of the importance entailed by world dependence on our oil.

The importance of Saudi oil appeared in the middle of this century, but the true extent of its undeniable global necessity emerged in the 1970s. The world then realised that it could never survive in its present form without Saudi oil, in the same way that Saudis can never dream of surviving in their present lifestyle without oil sales to the world. It is this mutual realisation which forms present relations between Saudi Arabia and most other countries. It is also the basis for all future Saudi economic planning and development.

For Saudi Arabia to continue to develop and prosper, oil exports must continue to flow from the Kingdom to the world. For this to happen, oil must flow freely at all times and at prices low enough to discourage discoveries of alternative oil supplies as well as alternative sources of energy. The present situation has been showing what can be described as a weakening of the Saudi position in the oil markets, with investments flowing in new oil-fields in many countries, and Saudi global market share falling over 30 per cent in real terms in the last 15 years. Saudi Arabia has been sacrificing its national interest in order to protect OPEC pricing and the production quotas of fellow members. This has led to lower overall petroleum prices, a diminishing OPEC market share, and gains by non-OPEC oil producers at an alarming rate. OPEC, from being a primary tool for Saudi affluence and prosperity, is fast becoming a burden on Saudi oil policy.

The realities of Saudi oil power, which have greatly contributed in making present-day Saudi Arabia wealthy, are very much still in existence. Saudi Arabia has a quarter of the world's oil reserves, one of the most advanced oil industries, with the lowest production costs for its crude. Saudi Arabia is reputed as a reliable oil supplier with the capability of increasing its production to meet the needs of its many global clients, in a manner which protects the international economic interests.

Much has been written about the development of the oil industry in Saudi Arabia, from the discovery of well Number 7 in Dhahran 60 years ago (1938) to the present situation. It is the story of hard work by courageous men and wise decisions by far-sighted leaders, a story of many struggles and victories. There is no reason to believe that the future is not going to be a continuation of this successful development process with Saudi Arabia continuing to lead the global hydro-carbon sector well into the next century.

We must also not under-estimate human scientific ingenuity and its capacity to discover other sources of energy which may become more attractive than oil in an economic and environmental sense. The day such discoveries make oil obsolete will spell disaster for Saudi Arabia, as oil is the undeniable major source of foreign currency income for the Kingdom at present as well as into the future. These discoveries have not been made yet and when made will take many years to supersede the supremacy of oil in the energy sector. This means that Saudi Arabia has the time to prepare itself economically for such a future scenario and many steps can be taken now to render oil even more attractive to users around the world. It is clearly in the interest of Saudi Arabia and its allies in the Gulf (Kuwait, UAE, Qatar, Bahrain and Oman), more than any other nations on earth, to have demand for oil continue and increase far into the future. It is therefore for Saudi Arabia to continue to lead all oil producers in the same supreme manner as has been happening in the past quarter of a century. There seems to be no alternative to that destiny for us Saudis and we should continue to apply it with the same global responsibility as has been our past behaviour, for therein lies the prosperity of our children.

3

The Rule of Al-Saud

SAUDI Arabia became a united and independent nation under the rule of Abdul-Aziz Al-Saud early in this century (1932). The conquests that marked this national birth and the steps that were implemented to reach full statehood have been well documented by many historians. What is important is to realise what we were prior to this process of unity and to therefore assess the enormous political, economic, and social gains that the creation of our country brought to our daily lives. From an assortment of disparate, poor and undeveloped territories controlled directly or through proxies by foreign powers, Abdul-Aziz Al-Saud forged the powerful independent nation that today carries his name. To say that he did this through the power of the sword would dramatically alter a complex historical process. He did use the sword, but in combination with political foresight, diplomatic prowess, Bedouin cunning, Islamic wisdom and ideology, to fulfill an outstanding achievement. When we look back at the last 90 years or more, we can sincerely judge this man's enormous will and vision. He united most of the Arabian Peninsula with scarce resources at his disposal and enormous odds against his success. But he did this with continued benevolence, truly wanting to better the lives of his fellow countrymen every step of the way. He has succeeded and we reap each passing day the fruits of his labour. We live at present in national wealth and affluence thanks to God, and then thanks to the unwavering belief and leadership of his servant, Abdul-Aziz Al-Saud, and his sons.

I will not go into the details of events that have resulted in contemporary Saudi Arabia, for they are historically well documented, but each one of them was a battle in its own right and a big step at its time. They involved a continuous process of gaining the trust and approval of the tribes, and through them the blessing and support of the entire Saudi population. We may consider the results of these events as a normal and expected part of our present daily life, may it be the wealth from oil or the education of our girls, but implementing each of these crucial actions was an act of vision and courage destined to improve the lives of all citizens on a long-term basis. History judges leaders for the results of their actions, yet these actions are formed by advice and execution. The successful leader is the one who chooses the right advisers, selects the most able men to implement his policies, and who is able to learn from them the skills which make his work more beneficial for his nation. It is therefore true to state that the success of Al-Saud and his sons is shared by the men who have served them and Saudi Arabia with such dedication, courage, ability, and who have found their just reward in their important participation in this outstanding national achievement.

The cocktail of ingredients that makes the rule of Al-Saud what it is today has certain common denominators. The most important one is certainly the wish to adhere all policies to Islam. Another parameter is the benevolence of the ruler in all his decisions – may they be of benefit to his people. The third common denominator to the rule of Al-Saud is the supremacy of the King in his decisions, balanced with the advice and wisdom of other members of the royal family.

It would be wrong to assume that Saudi Arabia is where it is today only because of coincidence and luck. Other nations in the Middle East have as many if not more resources, but because of various types of misrule, they suffer incredible political, economic and social problems. The success of leadership in Saudi Arabia is obvious, and it demonstrates the ability of the regime in often making the right decisions and quickly correcting mistakes when they occur before they have durable effects.

The rule of Al-Saud has faced over the years two types of threats. The internal threats are the first type, usually represented by those who oppose all types of economic and social progress, thereby fragmenting society and crucial growth. This has occurred repeatedly throughout this century, with the introduction of telephones, television, female education, etc. and in everyday actions that deeply affect the life and harmony of the population. This opposition has at times taken the form of armed insurrection, as represented by the Ikhwan Wars in the early years of the birth of Saudi Arabia (late 1920s) and the takeover of the Haram in Makkah (1979) by a radical fundamentalist group. This opposition has been caused by a mixture of genuine fear of change by an extreme fringe of our society, the greed and blind materialism of professional cronies, and the political opportunism of those interests that stir the emotions of the population in the hope that instability will bring them power and wealth.

The second type of threat to the rule of Al-Saud has been from external sources, as represented by the threat of Nasserism and socialism in the 1950s and 1960s, Iranian fundamentalism in the 1980s and 1990s, Iraqi aggression in the 1990s, etc. Such threats will always occur as Saudi Arabia has the two main assets desired by all nations in the Middle East and beyond, namely vast oil supplies and the holy

Islamic cities of Makkah and Madinah. He who controls these two assets is perceived to have gained influence over more than one billion Muslims worldwide and enormous clout over the world economy.

We must realise that such threats will always occur as fear and greed are unfortunate characteristics of human beings, and Saudi Arabia is one of the most valuable and seemingly accessible prizes in this world. We must also admit that Al-Saud have not only created this united country, but they have successfully and repeatedly defeated these internal and external threats, and have always continued to progress the country with pragmatism and balance. Their rule has always been firm, Islamically inspired, benevolent, and its success will continue well into the future if these elements remain as main instruments in government. So long as Al-Saud have the control of oil sources and the holy cities of Makkah and Madinah, and successfully enforce the self-discipline which has been a hallmark of their family rule, they will reign supreme over a united Saudi Arabia.

The legitimacy of Al-Saud lies in their Islamic form of rule, their benevolence, and their role as the fathers of modern Saudi Arabia. There exists no alternative to them at present and there is no logical need for an alternative to a continuously successful leadership. It must also be noted that their absence may disrupt the important balance which they have so successfully created and lead to the break-up of present-day Saudi Arabia and the end of our national dream. This possibility is perhaps the strongest asset of Al-Saud, now and into the future, as the entire population of the country understands that unity is the key to prosperity and happiness.

Part Two

What We Are

4

The People of the House

TO MANY people in this world, Saudi Arabia appears to be a nation of Bedouins who got lucky. We are perceived as simple people with a lot of money. The desert and camels are our symbols. Oil unfortunately flows from beneath our feet. The stereotype, as Hollywood and some media members have portrayed us, is a mixture of bearded Islamic terrorists and debauched gambling playboys. We are the lenders of last resort, the buyers of obsolete weapons, the recipients of the highest commissions, and the keepers of the largest harems. So much has been written, pictured, and said in that regard, that some of us even started believing it. One or two of our people have perhaps tried to live according to this legend of exotic 'macho' existence and they have only fuelled the imagination of those who claim to know our realities.

Legends can exist, but they will never replace the truth which ultimately prevails. In our case, truth has nothing to do with oil or money, truth is far from cinemas and casinos. Our truth lies deep in the chest of our people, it is the heart that beats and warms the Arabian desert. From the greenhouses of

Tabouk to the mountains of Asir, from Hail to Taif, from the desert dunes to the Haram (the holy mosque in Makkah), our simple reality has been discovered by all those who have sincerely searched for it.

Take away the money and the make-up and you will find a humane people. We are simple, this is true, but in our simplicity you will always find respect and hospitality. In us you will find dignity and a helping hand when you most need it. We will embrace you, but we will only do it in sincerity. We will never stab you in the back and we do not envy the bread on your table.

Compare the Saudi people to others with honesty and without envy. While the world suffers instances of moral breakdown, and the lines dividing right from wrong are confused by sheer power and material wealth, very few nations have continued to cling to pure and simple human decency as the basis for their policies and way of life. These are times when military oppression and occupation of the Palestinian people are sanctioned by the West as a normal right of existence of the Israelis. These are times when security agencies and terrorists work hand in hand to shape UN policies. These are times when arms merchants and paedophiles are protected by the same politicians in Europe. These are times when sex is more a part of advertising than loving relationships, and hunger coexists with 'butter mountains' and the 'mad cow' disease. Look at Saudi Arabia and its people then, and judge by real actions and true facts, not by fantasies and stereotypes.

We have our faults, like all humans do, but we sincerely try to correct them. We want to do good and to prevent evil. We try every day to make a positive difference, within our own house as well as with our neighbours. We are not angels, but which human truly is? In the balance sheet of nations, we are fortunately an asset, the good kids on the block. We believe that it is thanks to our religion and that it is the reality that no legend shall ever take from us.

We have never aggressed a weak neighbour and we do not invest our wealth in weapons of mass destruction. We will never interfere in your personal affairs and we do not wish you to mind ours. Oil has made us important to your life, but you must admit that we have handled this importance with responsibility and respect. Stand back and look at us, without envy and greed, and you will surely appreciate what you see. Forgive our faults and teach us how to correct them. Be patient with us and try to understand our ways and ideals. We mean well and we have always proven it. Take us the way we are and we promise never to disappoint you. Do not let our own weaknesses in communicating our realities alter the way you assess the truth of our existence and our relationship with you, for continuing to misunderstand us may only hurt your own strategic interests.

In the sands of Saudi Arabia, a prophet was once born, and he spread a message of respect and knowledge. We are his descendants, the 'Mohammedans' of the twentieth century. From our King to our schoolchildren, we are custodians of his legacy. Every day in our lives we strive to be like him. This is our simple reality and the secret of our being. When the lights go off, the sound is muted, and the truth prevails, this is what will remain for us. This is what we are. This is what we will always be.

5

The Free Market Economy

PRESENT-DAY Saudi Arabia is one of the largest market economies in the Middle East. There are no currency controls and no socialist dogma. Emphasis is placed on the private sector and its influence is encouraged to grow every day. This is perhaps due to Islamic doctrine which prevails supreme in the Kingdom. Islam prescribes that all wealth is owned by God, and the individual is an agent who is entrusted with portions of that wealth and who is then held accountable by the manner he or she uses it. Our economic model is also due to Western economic influence, especially that of the United States of America. This form of economy has led to the rise of rich and powerful business groups, usually in the form of family trading houses centered on the successes of a pioneering patriarch. The market economy has also led to the formation of an affluent and growing urban middle class representing the majority of consumers in the Kingdom.

The revenue from oil exports has certainly made such a free market possible as it created the necessary potential for economic growth and development. The existence of oil itself could have been an impetus for state control and economic centralisation, as the government has total ownership and management of this paramount source of national wealth. Government has instead created various instruments to encourage private sector participation in the economy. These range from overall reliance on Saudi nationals as formal representatives for all companies in Saudi Arabia to a multitude of soft loans available for private-sector development.

The policy for encouragement of private-sector involvement in the Saudi Arabian economy has been in place for several decades, fuelled by rising oil revenues and the need for national development. This policy is none the less gaining even more importance in this decade, as the nation realises its total reliance on oil revenues as the only true source of significant foreign currency earnings and the ensuing direct link between oil prices and the performance of the Saudi economy. The private sector is now encouraged to participate even more in the national economy and form new sources of revenue for the Kingdom as well as create additional employment opportunities for our growing population.

The government encourages private-sector growth through the implementation of mega infrastructural projects that have created excellent links between all parts of the country and other areas in the world, and enabled the development of profitable industries and quality services. A flourishing stock market is becoming the primary vehicle for privatisation of government corporations, thus increasing the national economic influence of the private sector.

A systematic policy of filtering oil revenues through a multitude of instruments to the private sector has always existed, but it is today gaining in importance and national priority. The successful application of these policies by the government is crucial to the future national growth of the private sector and the national economy. Chronically weaker oil prices and the expensive Gulf war have virtually eliminated our once large financial reserves and increased in a very serious way our national debt. An austerity programme is gaining in importance with efficiency emphasised at all levels of economic and social activities. The government is none the less attempting to strike a balance between the need to cut back on spending and the necessities of continued investment in an effort to soften the impact of a chronic economic recession. The efforts of the government will be vastly influenced in the medium term by oil prices, which are beyond the control of both the government and the private sector, and this unfortunately weakens economic confidence with direct effects on national investments, consumption and savings. This is a vicious circle and one of the realities of our today. It is also one of the serious threats to our children's tomorrow.

Saudi Arabia's successful economic development has certainly altered our demographic and social fabric. The growing importance of the middle class, the shift from the rural existence of farmers and Bedouins to the modern concept of industry and technical businesses, and the impact of enormous material wealth, these are all results that we are proud of as a nation. They contribute to our living comforts and form the basis for further future improvements. We must understand these changes in all their facets and their real influence on our social and national being, so that we are able to reform accordingly our handling of all our affairs in the most beneficial and least destabilising manner. We could thus maximise our gains as a society from the proven guidance and stability of Islam, without which we could never have reached where we are at present and without which there is no certain future for our society, whatever economic model we use as a nation.

6

The Achievement of Infrastructure

I T IS difficult for both Saudis and foreigners to stand back
and realise the true extent of infrastructural development
in the Kingdom over the last half a century. From virtually
nothing, Saudi Arabia now has a world-class infrastructure
network. The revenue from oil has been wisely invested into
the modernisation of the country in all possible sectors. The
funds expended are the highest per capita in the world over
the last quarter of a century and dwarf similar investments of
much admired high-growth economies such as Malaysia and
Mexico.

The development of the infrastructure has been complete
both in type and in geographic coverage. Saudi Arabia now
boasts a complete road network with over 80,000 modern
highway kilometres linking all corners of the country with the
rest of the world. Twenty-nine international and regional
airports are now operational, with the national airline Saudia
operating the largest aircraft fleet in the Middle East. The
Kingdom has the greatest water desalination capacity in the
world (over 2,000,000 cubic metres per day) and a fully
developed water-distribution network serving all population

centres. The electric generation capacity (approximately 20,000 MW) and the size of the national grid far surpass any other country per capita in the developing world. The telephone network is ultra-modern and covers the two million square kilometres land area of Saudi Arabia with excellent communications to the rest of the world. A functional state-subsidised health sector with thousands of hospital beds (in over 300 hospitals and 1,700 medical clinics) provides good medical services to all Saudis. Schools and universities (7 universities, 99 colleges, and 18,000 schools) have succeeded in fighting national illiteracy throughout the country. Affordable housing of good quality has been provided for a majority of the population. Television and radio stations from excellent competing native operators are in every Saudi household. City planning in most of the country's urban centres is used as an example of success by other Third World nations. These are concrete forms of development of national infrastructure which in reality give Saudi Arabia the basic requirements of a wealthy economy and a solid platform for future improvements.

The most important physical development for the Saudi economy has been the investment in the oil sector, which forms the basis for national wealth and income. Saudi Arabia has continuously improved its petroleum industry which is today considered amongst the most sophisticated and comprehensive in the world. The country is able to increase its production by nearly 35 per cent at short notice without damaging its plants and reserves. The Kingdom has reached efficient economies of scale in its oil sector with the lowest production cost and largest oil reserves in the world. Refining capacity is over 2,000,000 barrels per day and growing, in modern competitive facilities, increasing the national revenue derived from oil. It is the development of the oil sector which has made all other growth possible in the country and which will fuel all economic steps in Saudi Arabia's foreseeable future. There are still direct improvements that can be made to our oil industry, by increasing the recuperation rate of our reserves, and further expanding our distribution network inside and outside the country.

The sheer size and fast pace of government infrastructural development in the Kingdom has led to some mistakes in actual strategy and implementation. Clear examples of this are the so-called 'Fast Housing' programme, a large portion of which is yet to be distributed years after its completion as the types implemented clash with popular Saudi traditions, the leaking water distribution networks in many Saudi cities, and the storm drainage systems that fail haphazardly when it rains. We have also sometimes built too much of one thing and experienced shortages in other sectors. But these mistakes and misproportions are a minimal percentage of overall infrastructural development in Saudi Arabia and they are dwarfed by the reality of what was actually achieved in such a relatively short period. More experienced entities have made bigger miscalculations on comparatively less challenging developments, with the simple examples of the World Bank new headquarters building in Washington DC and Denver's new airport. This is no excuse for our failures, but it just shows that no human is infallible, however knowledgeable he may be. The secret is learning from mistakes and not repeating them too often, as this may wound national growth and development in a serious way.

The great future challenge for Saudi Arabia is not as much the extension of its infrastructure as the actual maintenance of what has been achieved. In times of weakness of the oil markets, the Kingdom has experienced difficulties in funding both routine and preventive maintenance in some infrastructural facilities due to the vast financial requirements involved. Success will only be achieved in the long term if we are able to balance our income with our actual needs and our priorities with our vast expectations. We must establish the financial methodology that will enable us to maintain and expand our infrastructural achievements and which gradually limits the paramount influence of oil prices on our economic development and our national existence. The challenges of tomorrow will magnify present problems, with water shortages always of primary concern, especially in view of a rapidly growing population. But the continued development of the oil industry, the expanding industrial base, the rising necessity for extensive job creation, and the sometimes unexpected requirements of the standard of living of the citizens in the twenty-first century, these are all considerations that Saudi Arabia must begin to address in its future planning for infrastructural development.

7

The Human Wealth

T HE greatest investment made using oil revenues over the past 50 years has been in the development of human resources. From a nation in vast majority illiterate, Saudi Arabia now counts hundreds of thousands of university graduates and some of the best technical cadres in the Middle East. This present situation has evolved through a dynamic and comprehensive policy to educate the nation in accordance with Islamic principles and to the highest international standards. The leadership realised early that Saudi Arabia had to acquire the technical knowledge in order to develop the country and maintain the high standard of living resulting from oil revenues. Saudis had to understand and learn to operate the technology they were acquiring if they were to modernise their country in a real manner.

Schools have been built in all population centres, both urban and rural, and universities in every major city. Education is free for every Saudi and a salary is disbursed for those who attend university. Technical colleges endeavour to train Saudis in the operation and maintenance of the infrastructure of the country. Thousands of Saudis attend Western institutions of higher learning every year under government scholarships. The success of this overall policy has been tremendous, with Saudis now in majority in most government institutions including the all important oil sector (Saudi Aramco) as well as state owned corporations such as Saudia and Sabic.

The most crucial development in the promotion of human resources in Saudi Arabia has been the decision to educate women on an equal level with men. Today, there are more girls at schools and universities in Saudi Arabia than boys and their results are academically getting better than their male counterparts (from below 10 per cent at the beginning of this century, the national literacy rate stands today at an average in excess of 65 per cent, with 80 per cent male and 50 per cent female). The biggest challenge in the future will be finding appropriate employment for these educated women in a balanced formula that both adheres to Islamic principles and meets the heightened expectations of this important portion of the population. In view of the five million foreign workers in the Kingdom and the limited employment opportunities available at present to our educated women, the issue of replacing some of the foreigners by male and female Saudis becomes a serious economic necessity. A 'Saudisation' strategy has been promoted by the government, but it is only partially successful with the private sector which logically seeks maximised profitability as an operational priority. Furthermore, Saudisation has not really addressed the sensitive issue of widespread female employment.

Another challenge to our future prosperity is finding suitable employment for all our university graduates and this will not always be easy. Other than the occasional preference of the private sector in employing foreigners for financial reasons, and because of their readiness to work in fields shunned by many Saudis, some of our university graduates will find it difficult to work in the private sector due to their specialisations. For example, thousands of Saudis have graduated in theology and Islamic studies and are perfect for jobs in the judiciary and religious establishments. But as these employment opportunities are filled, more and more of these fine Saudis find themselves outside the marketplace. This situation is dangerous as it can lead to economic hardship, frustration, and eventual political extremism. It is our national duty to find long-term economic solutions for our brothers, as it will cement further the cohesiveness of our society and ensure that the entire nation truly shares this Saudi dream.

As education permeates every level of our society, what is amazing is the level of religious consciousness of this learned class. Although many have studied abroad, these Saudis embrace Islam with passion and devotion. This can be explained by their increased understanding of their religion and Islam's encouragement of learning and knowledge. In the early years of Islam, a true revolution of knowledge overwhelmed the Muslim world from India to Spain, and made discoveries in medicine, algebra, astrology, etc. which were a major inspiration for the Renaissance in Europe and which still influence the life of the world today. Many Saudis hope that a new revival is on the way which will enable us to continue to develop our nation and participate in the promotion of prosperity and peace in the whole planet.

To achieve all our ambitions, we must understand that future improvements in our society can only happen if we continuously strive for excellence in our educational system and ingrained discipline in our very existence. Further economic growth is necessary to fuel our human wealth as the absence of good employment prospects will kill the ambition of our youth. Material wealth alone must never be confused with happiness, as has happened in certain Western societies. Economic affluence is necessary, but only if it is accompanied by moral depth, emotional equilibrium, intellectual satisfaction and social justice. Labour and humanity are the true basis for fuelling our drive for a better tomorrow and all our actions must be geared to encourage these noble elements of our national life.

Other Muslim nations, especially in South-East Asia, have achieved incredible economic growth and a true revival of Islamic thinking and belief, thanks to an excellence in their educational systems which has led to strong advances in medicine, science, legal studies, business management, etc. Saudi Arabia has achieved a lot over the past quarter of a century, but we have sincerely not reached the growth rate and depth of human development of countries such as Malaysia. It would be advisable for us to study these more successful models of education and human wealth development, as they are more favourably adapted to our social fabric than any Western examples that exist at present. With an even more accelerated rate of growth in the development of our human wealth, Saudi Arabia will hold the primary key towards future success and prosperity.

8

The Industrial Revolution

SAUDI Arabia has encouraged investment in industries in the hope that it would create employment, increase GDP figures, maximise revenue derived from oil wealth, and diminish the Kingdom's dependence on oil as the paramount source of national income. This encouragement has come in several forms. The first is direct government investment in strategic industries such as power generation, water desalination, and petrochemicals. The second is the provision of soft loans to the private sector to encourage the latter's participation in industrial ventures. The third form of encouragement comes in the provision of subsidised prices for services to industries (electricity, water, etc.). The fourth form is the provision of entire fully developed industrial parks within major cities, or as industrial cities themselves, with appropriate facilities for transport, communications and housing. The fifth form of government encouragement to industrialisation is in the imposition of higher duties to protect local producers of similar imported products. The last form of government encouragement to industry is the so-called off-set programme which obliges foreign companies selling military hardware to the Kingdom to reinvest the equivalent of 30 per cent of their sales value in technology projects in Saudi Arabia.

Due to these attractive incentives, Saudi Arabia today has the most extensive indigenous-owned industrial base per capita in the Middle East, with the exception of Israel. This successful development has been achieved through government-induced investments such as the various subsidiaries under the conglomerates of Sceco (electricity), Sabic (petrochemicals), Saudi Aramco (oil), etc. In these instances, government has been the primary mover in what are considered strategic industries as they rely heavily on petroleum as a raw material or as a source of energy. Sometimes, shares are sold on the stock exchange to the general public, as in the various Sceco and Sabic companies, but government retains a primary financial and management role.

The incentives offered to industrialists have also led to the establishment of thousands of privately owned factories of varying sizes producing all kinds of goods. These range from manufactured goods using petrochemicals as raw material, such as plastics and paints, to foods and beverages using local or imported raw materials. The range of products is extensive and of astonishingly good quality. The industrial plant is relatively new and always relying on the latest technologies. Many of these factories are able to compete favourably in the international market against established brands and corporations. An elite of industrialists exists at present in the Kingdom based on a wide spectrum of specialities and deep experience across the board. This certainly forms a strong basis for future expansion and will enable Saudi Arabia to enlarge its industrial base much further and decrease its reliance on oil as the main source of national income.

Some basic problems exist in the drive to industrialise Saudi Arabia, namely regarding foreign labour. A majority of factory workers, especially in the private sector, are foreign nationals employed because they are more competitively priced than Saudis and because the latter are not keen on this type of employment. Saudis seem to perceive a social stigma in working in certain jobs which are novel to our traditional way of life, but then so much of our present existence is made up of novelties that we have ably adapted to as a society. Government attempts to rectify this imbalance through the Saudisation programme have had limited success in the private industrial sector, and it is paramount to identify other instruments to rectify this problem, as the creation of employment for our growing population is of crucial national importance. A serious effort must be made to educate people on the true benefits of industrialisation and the good quality of life in that sector. We must teach our children these values if our nation is to transform itself into an industrial powerhouse. We must use our education system and the mass media within an organised campaign to market the attraction of the many incentives and advantages of these employment opportunities. We increasingly need these jobs for Saudis, and government must lead and assist if we are to succeed in securing them.

Custom duties to protect infant industries are not always applied to the full extent allowed by international trade treaties, therefore thwarting the very possibilities of industrialisation on an international scale. We must also evaluate our incentive packages to the entire industrial sector to maximise the attractive benefits and ensure that we can afford them as a nation. Our support for industrial development must be based on a correct analysis of realities and deep policies that enable both vertical and horizontal integration, with national profitability as the sole long-term goal.

Saudi Arabia is attractive as an industrial base for foreign investors due to the availability of cheap energy, plentiful raw materials, excellent infrastructure, government incentives, and a strategic geographic location. These foreign investors are important as they bring crucial technology, modern management, and additional financing which helps in the pursuit of further industrialisation in the Kingdom. We have attracted a lot of foreign investment in the country, and it has certainly played a crucial role in our successes to date, but some other nations have been doing relatively better than us with demonstrably less advantages to begin with. An example of this is Dubai, an emirate in the Gulf with a size much smaller than Riyadh, our capital, but with more than triple the trade and industry. We can go further and look at Singapore, the industrial city-state which ranks amongst the ten most industrialised nations on earth, after a concerted 30-year effort to reach such a status and no raw materials to fuel that success. We have our advantages and we must understand our mistakes.

If we sincerely wish to find alternative sources of national wealth other than oil, and if we believe that industry is a vast revenue centre, then there is no question that we can expand our present industrial base and that foreign investment will be very supportive to our future efforts. We must learn from the successes of others and understand how best to attract private and foreign investments, without which we will not achieve tomorrow's goals. Success will be further multiplied by the preservation of our heritage, our values, and our social structure, as each society is distinctive within the global sharing of common needs and purposes.

9

The Consumer Society

S AUDI Arabia is today a consumer society *par excellence.*
We rank as the largest importer of cars and video
entertainment systems per capita in the world. We are
amongst the ten highest spending nations on foreign tourism
although our population is a fraction of that of other
countries ranked. We have the largest number of executive
aircraft and yachts per capita, and the opulence of our houses
puts to shame Beverly Hills. Our supermarkets are astonish-
ing department stores of necessary and luxury foods, and our
jewellery shops exceed in stock value those in many industrialised nations. There is no question that we are a nation
that spends extravagantly in proportions only made possible
by the wealth derived from oil. There is also no question that
our spending can influence fashions, attract envy worldwide,
and provides us with some of the best services available
anywhere.

Once we assume these facts, we can start wondering how
much we can gain from our huge consumption as a society
and what will happen once the oil revenue decreases. Gains
are relative, depending on the type of consumption and its

source. If the product is imported, potential gain will be a fraction of locally produced alternatives. If the consumption is a necessity, it can be more beneficial to the consumer than a pure luxury. If the product consumed is affordable, it has more chances of lasting in the marketplace. In any capitalist and free-market society, consumption is regulated by income, supply, demand, fashion, etc. A necessary truck is perhaps more beneficial to a society than a passenger car, unless the car is a crucial mode of transportation. If either could be produced locally and economically exported, then it is certainly more profitable to that society. Immediate choices must be made, but they will have durable effects on our lives and economies.

The consumption of competitive services can lead to great improvements in social benefits, such as healthcare, and this may lead to a general improvement in the standard of living of the country once these services are affordable to all. By also providing free medical care and education to its citizens, the Saudi Arabian government has succeeded in encouraging private-sector health and education services of both high international standards and competitive costs. We must now find ways of ensuring that these services can be universally accessible to all users, both urban and in remote rural areas, depending on their choices and requirements, in a financially affordable manner at all times. Lower oil revenues have shown that these socially beneficial services have a capacity to lose quality and we must identify as a nation long-term economic solutions to this dilemma.

If a segment of our society consumes yachts in large numbers, and we neither produce them nor can maintain them ourselves, it is clear that we would not have been able to consume them without our vast oil revenues. If we build large palaces using locally produced cement and marble, we can presume that we can continue to build palaces even with lower oil revenues, if on a somewhat smaller scale. We must endeavour to consume more of what we produce ourselves and more of what we can afford to maintain. Once oil revenues diminish, and one day they will, we must be able to show our children what we have successfully built for them and which is truly beneficial to them. A daughter will appreciate her mother's jewellery, a son will be thankful for income property. It is debatable whether the consumption of Roquefort cheese or smoked salmon will help future generations, but they will quickly adapt to local goat cheese and canned tuna if they have been taught real values and flexibility.

What is crucial is that we are free to consume what we want and what we can afford at present. This is a right that many other Third-World nations have refused their citizens and we must be thankful for our freedom. We must realise that it is because of the flexibility and international character of Islam, the wealth from oil, and the benevolence of our leaders, that we are able to roam the world and live in luxury. We must plan to add more collective hard work, appreciation and savings to this list of influences, if our children are to enjoy these same luxuries far into the future.

Our fathers were not able to consume a fraction of what we have today. They lived a difficult existence where needs were simple and means very limited. They were proud and happy, not due to material satisfaction, but because of moral strength. We are the descendants of these valiant and generous Arabs, but we have been blessed with wealth and affluence. We should never forget our origins and our present financial capabilities should not divert us from our morality, our behaviour with others, and our future aspirations.

We must understand the envy of others for our wealth and how our prolific consumption can attract this envy. We must balance this with our necessity to import goods from nations that buy our oil to offset their trade deficits. We must improve our communications with them so that we truly portray our realities and not only our image of extravagant consumption.

We must ensure that we do not spend ourselves more than we can afford and that we can fully utilise what we are buying. At all times we must put our children's future in front of us, so that we can adequately visualise present actions in future contexts for continuing prosperity and success. Although this is a worldwide phenomenon, the enormous economic changes in Saudi Arabia make it a particularly crucial element of our thriving existence as a Muslim society in harmony with the entire planet.

10

The Agricultural Conquest

I F YOU happen to fly over the vast Saudi desert, you may see in the midst of the sand large green circles that seem to appear from nowhere and resemble some extra-terrestrial creation. Do not worry, you are only witnessing man's conquest of the desert in the form of wheat fields. In 20 years, Saudi Arabia has established itself as an important source of agricultural produce in the Middle East. The King-dom grows over two million tons of wheat each year and is the world's seventh largest exporter of the commodity. The King-dom is self-sufficient in poultry products and its greenhouses provide the population of the Gulf with succulent vegetables and Holland with fresh flowers. Meat production is rising and it covers at present nearly half the needs of the country. In the West, we hear of the Israeli miracle of turning the desert green. There is another miracle story in the Middle East, but we Saudis do not brag about it. Where the Israeli miracle was financed by the United States through donations, grants, aid, and technology transfers, and from the extensive water resources gained with the land conquests of its wars with Arab countries, ours has been financed by oil revenue. In both cases, hard work and perseverance have made the difference and the results are astounding.

Saudi Arabia has taken giant steps in the agricultural field, using government subsidies and soft loans to encourage investments in this sector. Great projects have been implemented to provide water through desalination and deep wells. Water distribution is extensive, enabling farmers to grow and prosper. Know-how and trained labour are plentiful, making for a sophisticated and profitable agricultural industry. High-grade fertilisers are produced locally by Safco and transport of production is extremely efficient by road, sea and air. Oil revenue has been invested to make the Kingdom a net food producer, it is to be hoped on a very long-term basis.

Agriculture is of strategic importance to Saudi Arabia, as it is the largest employment sector in the Kingdom, but only if continued growth can be sustained. Critics claim that only oil revenue keeps the sector alive as it helps in the expensive provision of water and the payment of government subsidies. But the critics are only partly right as subsidies for wheat alone support that commodity while other products are already competitive and independently profitable. Wheat requires a lot of water and it is clearly more expensive to grow in Saudi Arabia than in other locations where water is plentiful. It may be difficult for Saudi Arabia to continue growing so much wheat as water resources are rapidly depleting and may be better employed in other agricultural sectors. It is none the less very possible for the Kingdom to be self-sufficient in wheat on a long-term basis as we are depreciating our infrastructure and adding more efficient methods to our production. Our farmers must strive to get their wheat costs below international prices so that they can continue to make profits with minimum government subsidies. This is not an easy task if water is considered at its true cost. But then even the United States, the European Union, and Japan subsidise their farmers to keep them in business. It is a sovereign decision that has connotations of international importance. We must ensure that our children have the means to take such a decision in the future.

As a net result, the Saudi agricultural effort is successful and viable. It is ready for further growth and expansion, especially in the fields of greenhouses, meat production, and fishing. The latter has been a relatively ignored sector in comparison to overall growth in agriculture, especially when considering the thousands of kilometres of coastline represented by the country's shores and the rich fish resources of the Red Sea. Saudi Arabia must invest more in fishing and fish-farming as this requires very little of our precious sweet water resources and has the greatest future growth potential, especially in view of the delicious types (fish and shell fish) that our waters have become famous for.

We must target more mechanised methods of agricultural production as most of the labour in this sector is foreign. We must also encourage and train our youth to participate further in agriculture as this is a sector of great importance and future prospects. We must understand the technologies used and develop them further to serve our needs. We have to continuously face the reality of our geography and natural resources, where oil is plentiful and water rare, and where climatic temperatures are amongst the highest in the world. We must persevere in turning these characteristics of our nation into advantages for agricultural development, by accepting what is possible and ceasing what is difficult and uneconomic. Perhaps one day we will have truly conquered the desert and extracted from it abundant green gold in addition to the black version that is crucial for our present prosperity.

11

The Economic Expectations

THE population of Saudi Arabia lives in great affluence. Oil revenues and benevolent government policies have created comforts that exceed those found in many rich and developed nations. Every Saudi can expect good and free healthcare services from his birth to his death. He can expect free education from primary school to the doctorate degree. The Saudi does not pay any formal taxes, and he can quite easily find an adequate job. He will have one car or more and an air-conditioned home with all modern luxuries. Many Saudi homes have at least one foreign servant, in addition to a driver to take the children to school and Madame on her errands. Our population has become used to subsidised goods and services such as cheap fuel, electricity and water. Duties on imported goods are very low by Middle-East standards and products are plentiful. Our shops are accessible to all and food outlets are of high international quality. We like to travel in our vacations in search of new experiences and good weather. The inflation rate in the country is low and the Saudi Riyal is as stable as the US dollar. Security and peace of mind are benefits for all citizens. Saudis live in an economic paradise when compared to most other nations.

With this relatively new affluence, which did not exist 50 years ago, Saudis have grown expectations which they now consider as virtual necessities. We expect the standard of living which we have. We consider free education and healthcare as normal. We assume that we will always have good jobs and subsidised services. We never expect to pay any taxes and we dislike import duties. These are luxuries which have become an integral part of our daily lives and which are visualised as basic to our future aspirations. They are in reality abnormalities that do not exist in other nations, certainly not developed and wealthy Western countries that already experience difficulties in financially maintaining their more limited social benefits.

The three features which have shaped our existence, namely Islam, oil, and Al-Saud, have ensured our affluence. Alterations in any of these characteristics could lead to a change in our standard of living and possible disappointments in our level of expectations. A fundamental change in the applications of Islam, a dramatic lowering in the levels of oil revenues, and a serious instability to the rule of Al-Saud, are all possibilities that will drastically change our way of life. We should never underestimate the influence of Islam on our social fabric and being. We have to fully comprehend the paramount benefits of oil on our economy. We must realise that our rulers have always aimed with success at the policies which have built our present prosperity and security. These are the true reasons for our affluence and we must endeavour to value and preserve them for our children's future.

Events such as the takeover of the Haram (holy mosque) in Makkah, or the cash crunch following the Gulf War, are but brief glimpses of possibilities that can shake our existence and destroy our national achievements. They do not indicate that we have fundamental weaknesses as much as they highlight that we are not immune to dramatic changes in the future. We must therefore concentrate our efforts as a nation at strengthening those characteristics that shape so clearly our existence and clarifying our own responsibilities and expectations. We must always remember our roots and mind our behaviour towards others less fortunate than we are. We must teach our children the true values of God, King and Country, and the benefits that these values have on their daily lives. We must explain to them our realities so that they can build for themselves and their children a better tomorrow.

We are a nation of the desert where life was tough for centuries. Our fathers had to strive to support their simple existence. They became famous for their humanity and generosity. We face none of these difficulties, but we must always remember the past and learn from our own experience. We must understand what we have achieved in comparison to our past as well as relative to other nations, and where we wish to go from here. We must determine the responsibilities of each one of us and the relationships between us. We have to analyse our expectations and concentrate on the priorities that truly influence our being, so that shortfalls do not affect our prosperity as a nation. We must understand our mistakes so that we do not repeat them in the future. We should modify our behaviour in a manner that will improve our overall performance and bring us even closer to our Islamic values. We have to accept that what we have is a real blessing and that we can influence our future happiness through our own actions. It is in this way that we are able to continue to build the Saudi dream for ourselves and the following generations.

12

The Principles of Power

THE Al-Saud reign relies on several basic principles in governing the country. The most important of these principles is the will to apply the Sharia (Islamic law) in all aspects of daily life and constitutional behaviour. A second principle is the benevolence of policies to benefit the entire population and seek national prosperity on a long-term basis. The third principle is the cohesion and unity of what was not so long ago a purely tribal and fragmented society. The fourth principle is the safeguarding of the nation from external and internal threats to its sovereignty and future independence. Al-Saud fully understand that the correct application of these principles ensures the prosperity of the nation and the strong continuity of the reign of the royal family.

Al-Saud have always been in alliance with the Wahabi religious establishment, which advocates strict adherence to Islamic principles in all facets of life. This has meant that policies and reforms are set in accordance with the Sharia, which is the law applied in Saudi Arabia. Where this has meant conservatism in approach, it has in no way stopped the incredible development that has occurred in the Kingdom.

Throughout the modernisation process, each step has been analysed for its adherence to Islamic doctrine and its possible effects on our society. At times, certain fundamentalist sections of the religious establishment have opposed certain reforms out of fear that they may have negative results on the population and Islam in the country. None the less, these reforms have been implemented by the rulers for their clear positive effects, in a manner that both protected the adaptable character of Islam and demonstrated the assurance and strength of the ruler. The result is a society that is pious, cohesive, technically aware, and ready for further growth. It is the balance that has been achieved between the strict application of Islamic scriptures and fast modernisation that has made the success of the rule of Al-Saud and benefited so greatly our society. It is this balance which will make future development a natural course of action which we can all look forward to.

Some critics have voiced their apprehension at the power which the religious establishment has been exercising and how it can compete with the rule of Al-Saud. Critics claim that important reforms are shelved because of the veto of the fundamentalists. This may have occurred in the past half a century, since the creation of the Kingdom of Saudi Arabia, but it has never thwarted lasting development and the rule of Al-Saud has at all times prevailed because it is supreme. Al-Saud rely on Islam out of belief and because this is the wish of the great majority of the population of the country. The powers of the religious establishment are given to it by the ruler out of respect for Islam, the sincerity of religious scholars, and by the King's need for theological advice. These powers can be regulated and curtailed to a certain degree at the wish of Al-Saud, as has been demonstrated on several occasions in the past when fundamentalism had attempted to halt development (the introduction of the telephone, television, female education, etc.).

Al-Saud have always aimed at the development of the country in a manner that brings prosperity to a great majority of the population. This benevolent policy has achieved tremendous results in the Kingdom and has strengthened the rule and very existence of the royal family. The affluence which our citizens enjoy is to a great extent a product of the correct decisions of Al-Saud, as is demonstrated by the sad situation in other oil rich but poorly governed countries such as Iraq, Iran, and Algeria. Our prosperity adds further legitimacy to the rule of Al-Saud, who have truly created the Kingdom of Saudi Arabia and managed its development so successfully.

We started the century as a tribal society, but tribal restraints have been diminished by migration to the large cities and economic development. Nevertheless, tribalism is still an important consideration in our lives, especially in matters pertaining to the armed forces and support for the royal family. Growth in development and the completion of important infrastructural projects such as roads and telecommunications have broken down the barriers between regions that were not so long ago different countries. We must be objective and admit that many of us still view each other in veiled terms of tribal origins, with so-called outsiders sometimes regarded suspiciously, and this still influences employment and social relations. But where this is an influence, it is certainly not the rule, and we hope that time will enable us all to discard these petty racial complexes, for this weakens our national identity, unity and our total adherence to Islam.

Due to the wealth from oil and the importance of Makkah and Madinah, Saudi Arabia will always face threats. Other countries will envy us and some individuals will covet the power of Al-Saud. He who controls Saudi Arabia has his hands on a unique jewel, the prize of ultimate religious importance and fabulous monetary wealth. But the achievement of national prosperity and international respect takes wise leadership, and this is what Al-Saud have successfully implemented in Saudi Arabia and which many other leaders have failed to bring about elsewhere. This wise management must sometimes deal with difficult situations which threaten the nation and its prosperity, but the track record shows that difficulties can be surmounted and that the population has always surrounded the leadership with loyalty and support in times of crisis. Saudi Arabia can prevail against its hidden enemies, but it must be cautious, united, and prepared. Those who threaten the country are not only targeting the power of the royal family but our national existence and wealth. Their success could mean our collective loss and the possible end of our prosperity. We do not wish a Saddam Hussein or a Khomeini to destroy our lives and we will fight in support of our King to prevent such a disaster. This is a fact that our King knows very well.

13

The Tools of Government

A L-SAUD rely on several tools in governing the Kingdom. The King reigns supreme over all and his decision
once taken is final. But in his supremacy, the King
depends on others in his family and among the population to
formulate and execute policies which must always adhere to
Islamic principles. The application of these policies is then
implemented in an organised and efficient manner as has
been demonstrated throughout this century.

The King ultimately controls the three branches of government, namely the executive, represented by the Cabinet of
Ministers, the legislative, represented by both the Majlis Al-
Shoura (the consultative council) and Al-Irshad wal Fatwa
(religious advisory council) and the judiciary, represented by
the religious and commercial courts. He presides over all
ministerial meetings as Prime Minister, appoints all members
of the consultative council and religious leadership, and he
must confirm all judiciary decisions. In his supreme role, the
King has to formulate decisions based on the principles of
power applied by Al-Saud, the aspirations and beliefs of the
population, and the social and geopolitical needs of Saudi

Arabia. Sometimes, in view of the fast economic development of the country and the environment in which it evolved over the last 50 years, managing the government must have constituted a balancing act requiring a combination of a firm grasp, flexibility in approach, and very wise vision. The results achieved mark the magnitude of the success of this system of government and the management abilities of its administrators.

The executive branch of government is not only constituted by the various ministries, but also includes the local administrations in each region of the country, namely the Imarat (governorships), which are usually headed by royal Princes. This means that government is not only present under technical departments which cover all aspects of our daily lives, but also on a geographic and demographic coverage that caters to our needs and is supposed to regulate inefficiencies in administration. This system enables the King, to whom all ministers and governors report, to have a first-hand perspective of the real condition and feelings of the population, as every Saudi has direct access to all government officials through the Majlis (open house) system of representation.

The legislative branch of government has been reformed in the last few years through the appointment by the King of a consultative council, to revise legislation and recommend modifications to the King and his government. All legislation has to adhere to Islamic doctrine and eventually receive the approval of the religious advisory council, so that a form of consensus is achieved. As this system in its reformed mode is fairly new, its results are not established in a clear manner. But as the recent reforms encompassed by the creation of the consultative council are only an improvement of the established legislative practices that were applied in the past, there seems to be a good chance that performance in producing improved legislation will flourish in the future. The

consultative council is constituted by highly educated technocrats with a deep understanding of the issues they must
analyse and sometimes reform. They are chosen by the King
to represent the various segments of our society, so that their
advice is a mirror of the aspirations and vision of the entire
nation. Their mission and the true extent of their powers
must be clarified further in the near future, for their novel
role is to effectively benefit the people of Saudi Arabia within
the present governing framework.

Critics say that the creation of the consultative council does
not go far enough in democratising the country and its
institutions, as members are directly appointed by the King
and are not elected by the population. Such criticism is unfair
in that it fails to understand the representative character of
the government in Saudi Arabia, the efficiencies of the Majlis
form of accessibility by all to the ruler, and the quality and
dedication of the members of the consultative council. The
test will come in the future when the actual performance of
the legislative bodies can be impartially assessed based on
results and their repercussions on our daily lives. It is at
present questionable if elections could have resulted in a
better Majlis Al-Shoura, especially as we Saudis are still
tribal in outlook, with no experience in electing able representatives for legislative posts. Such experience will take years
of education to permeate our society and must be integrated
under clear Islamic principles into our system of government.
Democracy has beautiful connotations of equality and justice,
but only if it is correctly applied. Islam has clear democratic
principles ingrained in its doctrine, such as the equality of all
before the law and the respect of human rights. It is therefore
in the application of true Islamic principles at all times that we
will improve our democratic adherence in life as a way to
prosper in the future.

The judiciary applies the Sharia (Islamic law) in all its
functions and rulings, and this covers all citizens and resi-

dents in the country. Killing is punished by death, as is terrorism, drug smuggling, and the rape of women and children. Amnesty International may think that this is a cruel approach to crime prevention, but it is the structured approach that our religion indicates, and the low crime rate in the Kingdom is proof that this strict legal policy is successful and popular. It is for us as Saudis to ensure that equality is always applied for all by the judiciary, as this is a central characteristic of Islam and any compromise on this issue will greatly affect us socially and emotionally. The King stands as the ultimate arbitrator in case of any failures or weaknesses in the performance of the judiciary, and this has usually proven to be an effective control function that has benefited the country and its people. It is crucial that such controls are strengthened in the future, perhaps with the help of the Majlis Al-Shoura, as the judiciary has social and religious connotations with an enormous direct effect on our daily lives.

14

The Sword that Shines

I N THEIR rule, Al-Saud rely on various security measures to ensure peace at the borders and within. These range from the Armed Forces, the National Guard, the Border and Coast Guard, the police units, Civil Defence, Al-Mabahith Al-Aama (the General Investigation Bureau), Al-Itisalat Al-Kharijia (the Foreign Intelligence Service) and Heyat Al-Amr Bil Maarouf Wal Nahi An Al-Munkar (the Religious Police). This may seem like a long list, but with only one exception (the Religious Police) it is identical to the security measures of most Western nations. The result is a nation that is peaceful by international standards, with a very low crime rate, in a turbulent region where serious crimes are definitely on the rise.

The Armed Forces, National Guard, Border and Coast Guard, and Foreign Intelligence Service are all responsible for the protection of the country from outside threats. They are extremely well equipped, highly trained, and they have demonstrated their capabilities against real military threats from countries such as Iran and Iraq. Saudis constitute all combat units with some foreign support in training and maintenance. These powerful military outfits are the descendants of the Bedouin army that united the country over 70 years ago, but this is where the comparison stops. The present military force has to rely on expensive technology to counter serious opponents with large populations and armies and unfriendly intentions towards the Kingdom. Due to its high-tech nature, the Saudi military has had to absorb new equipment and defence systems in record time, with serious obstacles imposed on effective supplies for many years by Israel and its infinite influence on the US government. The cost of this defence strategy has been very high, but so are the threats to oil supplies and national independence which have made our present prosperity possible.

I have often read foreign media reports on the weaknesses of the Saudi military and its reliance on foreign combat units to implement its defence mission. Until the surprise Iraqi invasion of Kuwait, there were no foreign combat units in the Kingdom and these arrived from dozens of nations after Saddam Hussein's crazy action. It was clear that Saudi Arabia did not have the military capacity to liberate Kuwait on its own against the large, experienced, and aggressive Iraqi Presidential Guard divisions. In earlier threats, it was Saudi pilots flying Royal Saudi Air Force F-15 fighters that downed Iranian combat aircraft violating Saudi airspace near our oil fields. Foreign nationals were used for support functions in maintenance and training, but never as combat forces before the Gulf War. Due to the recent experience of that sad event (1990), the US and other Western powers now keep some equipment and troops in the Kingdom, as a safety precaution against future threats to the Saudi oil supply to the world. The presence of these foreign forces has been strongly criticised by some religious and nationalist elements in the country as an infringement on Saudi sovereignty and independence, and a threat to Islam. This is because the US is perceived by many people in Saudi Arabia and the Middle East region as the main political, economic, and military support for Israeli aggression against Arabs in general, and Palestinians in particular. This criticism is often blinded by xenophobia, leading to bloody terrorist attacks that appear to be aimed at foreigners, but it ignores the disastrous consequences on our lives of a successful foreign aggression on the Kingdom. I sometimes feel that such criticism is used as an excuse to attack the rule of Al-Saud, as if the fate of the population is different from the fate of its rulers. Try explaining this to the people of Kuwait who suffered national rape and pillage because a tyrant neighbour claimed to dislike Kuwaiti rulers.

On the internal front, the Saudi security services have been successful in fighting crime and ensuring social peace. We are able to live in complete safety and there are none of the excesses that permeate human life in neighbouring countries. Saudis do not disappear at night from their houses, and it is certainly not the common practice of our police to shoot at young rock-throwing demonstrators and destroy their houses. Our security services are strong and efficient, and they have to a great extent successfully limited terrorism and banditry in the country, when other Middle-East nations have been deeply wounded by these now fashionable diseases. Theft is rare in Saudi Arabia in comparison with many other nations. It is true that we severely punish culprits, but this is based on Islamic law and popular desire. Islam strongly stresses justice for all and we must as a nation guarantee that this is always an integral part of our lives.

Most of the criticism within the Kingdom is directed against members of the Religious Police and their sometimes heavy-handed approach to the upholding of public morals. We must understand that the Religious Police are unique to Saudi Arabia and are as much a remnant of our past as a portion of our future. They have an important role to play in the fight against alcohol and drugs which have unfortunately attacked our social fabric and youth. They must monitor the terrorist activities of certain fundamentalist fringes of our society, as they may be better able to comprehend the true causes of their bloody and destabilising actions. We must find ways to increase the effectiveness of our religious police in its many beneficial functions and limit some of the excesses that have troubled many Saudis. We must ensure that all members of the Religious Police are in tune with national needs and sentiments, that they implement their functions with professionalism and sincerity, and that they do not become a negative reaction to development and prosperity. We Saudis must work with the religious establishment to fight crime and immorality, as our success will guarantee our future prosperity and social harmony in all the country.

It is the wise use of the sword that establishes peace and security in a nation. There must also be strong morality, preparedness, and social discipline, and this is what Islam provides for us. A low crime rate is an immense contribution to the happiness and high standard of living of a nation. The capability to face regional threats is a reality which we must confront objectively and plan for. The cost of such a defence must be studied carefully and modified according to our needs and capabilities, without waste, inefficiencies and the diminishment of our independence. Popular harmony, the will of the nation to defend itself, and the respect of human rights are all essential ingredients of Islam, and these are strongly aided by the notion of justice for all. We must ensure that this is part and parcel of the future, as the happiness, prosperity, and independence of our children will be based on it.

15

The Management of Finance

THE vast oil revenue which has flooded Saudi Arabia since the 1950s has been managed in a manner which has resulted in our present prosperity and affluence. It has enabled government plans to be implemented successfully and has efficiently circulated money in the economy. In its present form, the management of government revenue has become integrated with the overall financial apparatus in the country and this has proven to be crucial in national daily cash-flow requirements and allocations. It is the analysis of this financial system and its true efficiency which will help us evaluate its actual performance and to assess objectively any modifications that may have to be implemented to protect the economic future of our children.

The government manages national revenue through the Ministry of Finance, which in turn monitors the Saudi Arabian Monetary Agency (SAMA, our central bank) and the expenditure of all government departments. SAMA controls all banking activities in the country, issues and supports the Saudi Riyal (our currency), and holds all national financial reserves. All government revenues and expenditures are

assessed within the framework of a national budget. This
budget is prepared annually by the Ministry of Finance, with
input from all government departments.

SAMA regulates an extensive list of financially powerful
banks that are registered in Saudi Arabia. These are either
fully Saudi-owned (National Commercial Bank, Al-Rajhi
Bank, Al-Riyadh Bank), or in joint-venture with foreign
partners (Saudi-American Bank, Al-Bank Al-Saudi Al-Fransi,
Al-Bank Al-Saudi Al-Hollandi, Saudi-British Bank, Saudi Investment Bank, Bank Al-Jazirah, Saudi United Commercial
Bank, Saudi Cairo Bank, and Arab Bank). Some of these are
considered amongst the largest and most profitable Middle-
East financial institutions and they play a primary role in
Saudi daily life. They take deposits, give loans, issue credit
cards, provide letters of credit and guarantees, and all other
modern banking activities. Their operations are fully auto-
mated to the highest international standards. They have
effective representations in most countries in the world,
either through subsidiaries or through representations with
major foreign banks. They have a good reputation and they
are successful in achieving many of their goals by effectively
utilising the financial freedoms provided by the Saudi system
of government.

As effective as the Saudi banking apparatus has proven to
be, with a constantly stable currency pegged to the US dollar,
it still has weaknesses in some aspects of its performance.
Saudi banks do not easily provide project financing and
mortgages by claiming that they are not adequately protected
by the applied legal practices in the Kingdom, and certain
SAMA regulations. A review of this problem is urgent and
necessary as the privatisation programme envisioned by the
Saudi government will mean added emphasis on the banking
sector in the investment and credit fields, and any weaknesses
in local banking performance will have a compounded effect
on the entire national economy. All future modifications in

banking activities must bear in mind the growing importance of the Stock Exchange and the protection of banks from speculation and over-leveraging in their operations, as well as the elimination of any existing regulations that may be impeding healthy growth and prosperity.

There is a whole sector of the banking industry, namely Islamic banking, that is not adequately regulated or supported. Several Islamic Banks operate in the Kingdom under foreign registration (mostly Bahrain) or normal Saudi banking licences not always fully compatible with their activities. As this sector is growing in importance, it is essential that appropriate legislation is implemented to regulate all Islamic banking activities in Saudi Arabia and to support them in an organised manner that protects shareholders, depositors, and creditors. This will promote and enhance Islamic banking which will one day form an important segment of our financial management system, once it has matured on strong foundations.

In its management of the national budget, the Ministry of Finance is responsible for all government revenue and expenditure. With a chronic budget deficit, government has been borrowing in the international and local financial markets through bond issues, oil barter contracts, and direct export credits for government contracts, to finance the deficit. This is a normal practice in international financial circles, but it must always be within clear limits which do not disturb the money supply and diminish the availability of funds to the private sector. Government debt must always remain in manageable proportions and within transparent procedures to enable it to be repaid through improved future revenues and diminished expenditures, without upsetting the country's credibility and credit worthiness. We should not reach points of no return on our national debt, like the time bomb that burdens at present the US economy, as our abilities are not as sophisticated or developed as most Western nations. It is furthermore more wise for Saudi Arabia to spend less of its oil revenue and build a strong financial reserve, rather than rush expenditure and be threatened with a huge national debt.

An essential ingredient in the management of any successful economy is its credibility. Saudi Arabia is respected in all international financial forums because of its enormous oil wealth and the large economic needs of the Kingdom. The delays in payments to contractors and the 10 per cent final payments on government projects are frequent occurrences which hurt market confidence, increase project costs across the board, and wound the paramount reputation of the government as the guarantor of last resort. They are not part of a concerted government policy, as some critics claim, but are a product of bad habits, the misjudgement of national priorities, and weak financial management of cash flow by some government officials who continue to ignore the seriousness of this 'unofficial' local debt. The whole deficit financing strategy must be analysed and modified so that it can be implemented in an efficient manner which does not harm the national economy, the growth of the supply of money necessary for development, and the faith which the world has in our government, its overall management of national finances, and its complete fulfilment of all its promises. The Ministry of Finance has excellent technocrats both capable and worthy of addressing these issues in a manner that will eradicate all negative ramifications on the national economy. SAMA must be totally independent of the Ministry of Finance, and behave at all times as the central bank which it was designed to be, if we wish to see continued efficiency and stability in our financial system in the future.

The fact that there is room for improvement in an already advanced and successful financial sector augurs well for the future. Saudi Arabia is the premier example of achievement in developing nations and any improvements we can make will translate in maximised efficiency and more prosperity.

We should thus analyse our financial management system carefully, learn from our past mistakes, align our expenditure within our national needs, and gear our efforts towards future growth and development in a manner which squeezes all benefits from every dollar we earn and limits the many possibilities for waste.

16

The Foreign Policy

SAUDI foreign policy has been based on four firm precepts, namely Islam, Arabism, oil, and the defence of the nation. These are characteristics that have created and totally affected the Kingdom's foreign policy since its inception. Oil only rose in importance in the late 1940s, at which time Saudi Arabia was propelled on to the world stage. But the Kingdom was formed at the beginning of the twentieth century, when oil was not yet discovered under the Saudi sands. Saudi Arabia was founded by the vision of one man, Abdul-Aziz Al-Saud, supported by the aspirations of the population and based on Islamic doctrine. The young nation was purely Arab in identity and being. The religious assets of Makkah and Madinah, and the advent later on of oil, increased potential and real foreign risks. The country found itself threatened on several fronts, and it had to find immediate and lasting solutions to all foreign challenges.

To tackle threats, alliances are necessary and effective strategies must prevail. A clear and precise understanding of all obstacles must exist so that policies correctly reflect targets and needs. Saudi foreign policy has successfully dealt with threats and it has been instrumental in the country's present prosperity. In the Islamic arena, Saudi Arabia holds a leading role equivalent to its importance (the holy cities), but beyond the small size of its population (1 per cent of all Muslims are Saudis). The Islamic World League and the Islamic Development Bank are based in Saudi Arabia, and the Kingdom has been an effective leader in the defence of Islamic interests in human tragedies from Afghanistan to Bosnia.

Saudi Arabia has played a leading role in Arab causes, hoping to achieve consensus and unity. The Kingdom is the largest financial donor to the Palestinians, with real actions instead of the many empty words of others. Its policies have always stressed moderation and balance in the hope that the Arab nation will eventually rid itself from the vestiges of colonialism and misrule and unite in front of all challenges in word and deed, in a manner that benefits all Arabs and the world. It is with this aspiration that Saudi Arabia deals with other Arab nations within the Arab League as well as the Gulf Co-operation Council. Throughout history, events have a direct effect on all plans, and the actions of famous men such as Jamal Abdel-Nasser and Saddam Hussein have adversely affected the very Arab unity which they claimed to promote. Whether these actions were badly conceived or based on false pretences is open to debate, but they have resulted in disaster for the Arab nation as they have exposed our differences and weaknesses. The bill for adventurism has been heavy and Saudi Arabia has always had to pay in financial and moral support for the mistakes of others. This is the price of Arabism, a natural phenomenon so misunderstood by Arabs themselves and their respective powerful foreign allies.

We must mention the now virtually defunct communist ideal and its efforts for world revolution and domination. Although the Soviet Union was the first powerful nation to recognise independent Saudi Arabia, the feeling was never mutual and Saudi Arabia was always communism's greatest

enemy. Some observers assumed that Saudi Arabia was firm in
its opposition to the international socialist dream because of
the position of our Western allies who both bought our oil
and fought communism relentlessly until its most powerful
proponent was defeated economically. This assumption is
wrong, as the reasons for Saudi opposition to communism are
much more fundamental. Saudi Arabia regards communist
ideology as the enemy of Islam, the only religion that accepts
all other faiths that advocate one God, while communism is
based on pure atheism. Saudi Arabia can never accept any
real co-operation with a political system which is totally alien
to our beliefs and way of life. This opposition was economically costly because of the importance of oil exports to both
Saudi Arabia and the Soviet Union, and the absolute lack of
co-ordination on this important issue between the two
countries.

Oil has been both a tool and an asset which must be
protected in the application of Saudi foreign policy. It is a
political tool in promoting causes important to the Kingdom,
such as in the imposition of the oil embargo in 1973 to assist
the Arab political struggle against Israel and force a just and
peaceful settlement for all in the Middle East. It is an asset
which must be protected, such as in the dramatic increases in
Saudi oil production after the Iranian Revolution (1978) and
the Iraqi invasion of Kuwait (1991). Oil's incredible importance makes it politically potent, but prosperity can only be
assured if buyers are plentiful, secure in their supplies, and if
we control as a nation the marketing of this commodity. Saudi
oil policy has always aimed at fair pricing and uninterrupted
production, and this has greatly contributed to the country's
international importance and its economic prosperity. Oil is
also the main reason for the strong Saudi–United States
alliance, as it is clear that both nations need each other. This
mutual economic reliance was at times strengthened by the
global fight against communism, and at other times weak-

ened by the unconditional USA support for Israel, and the latter's clear and continuing oppression of the Palestinian people and their basic human rights. The USA support for Israel is the main reason for the mistrust which Arabs in general feel towards the world's greatest power, and which has been translated by some extremists in Saudi Arabia into terrorist bombings against USA military targets in the Kingdom.

The Palestinian tragedy has directly affected the politics and stability of the entire Middle East since the Second World War. In the last four years, the delightful prospects for lasting peace have overwhelmed us all, but the road is still long, mistrust is prevalent, and wounds run deep. Saudi Arabia has been directly involved because of Jerusalem, which holds enormous religious importance to all Muslims. The Saudi position has always been supportive of the Palestinians in their demands for their own independent state, and it emphasised that peace must be negotiated and decided by the Palestinian people and their legitimate representatives. No comprehensive peace could be implemented without the fair settlement of all issues with all participants, including the Golan Heights, Southern Lebanon, the right of refugees to return to their homeland, comprehensive security for all, the right of the Israelis to live in complete safety and prosperity within recognised international borders, and the paramount issue of holy Jerusalem. It is hoped that true and just peace will be reached soon so that the blind hatred and the horrible killings can cease, and the healing process will finally begin for all in the Middle East.

We are a peaceful people, with no ill-feeling towards any other nation. Our record in international relations remains unblemished throughout the twentieth century. But this unfortunately does not mean that we can relax and expect others to behave peacefully like us. It is to be expected that foreign threats will continue to plague the Kingdom and its future. Oil wealth and religious importance are too attractive to some of our neighbours and a few world powers. There will always be plots to counter and challenges to address. This is the price we must pay for our affluence and prosperity. If we wish to preserve our sovereignty and independence, then we must always be prepared to defend ourselves and repel our opponents. Saudi Arabia must never be an easy prize for anyone. We should always maintain the necessary alliances, pack the most potent armaments, and build the most efficient national army, to dissuade the most vicious potential enemies from the thought of ever attacking us. This is the cost we must pay for our children's happiness and peace of mind.

17

The Cancers of Our Time

MODERN times have brought us comforts and affluence, and they have simplified and lengthened our lives. The world is supposedly a better place to live in, in this age of jet travel, sophisticated medical care and the Internet. Improved communications and more extensive trade ties have brought people closer together, hopefully leading to global understanding and harmony. Yet wars still occur on all continents with higher casualties, thanks to the increased sophistication of weapons, and racism is prevalent deep in many people's hearts. The difficulties of yesterday have changed and present problems come in a different guise. They occur because of the weakness of human beings, functioning adversely within the fabric of modern society. They are the cancers that eat away at the fringes of our daily lives and our social balance, and which can overwhelm us if we do not fight them relentlessly and uproot them from our existence.

Examples of these social cancers abound in our world. Narcotics have taken over entire countries and their cartels behave internationally as efficient and powerful multi-nationals. Corruption has caused the fall of diverse governments from Italy to Japan, and makes business dealings with countries such as Nigeria an unsavoury gamble. Gangs have turned certain American cities into battlefields, and the family unit is losing its cohesiveness in the West. Extremism is on the rise, and terrorism has shaken powerful nations and indiscriminately targeted the innocent bystanders. Civilisation is being exposed to these various woes which are caused by the increased materialism of our daily lives and the weakening of the moral fabric. Their magnitude is increased by the rising importance of the media and the ills of unemployment, poverty and social injustice.

Saudi Arabia has been lucky when compared to the many other nations which have been directly devastated by these cancers. Drug and alcohol addiction is on the rise in the Kingdom, but it is minute by international standards. Crime is an issue, but only because we have enjoyed for a long time a crime-free life that we are afraid to lose. (As an example, the murder rate per capita in the USA is over 20 times the per capita rate in Saudi Arabia.) Extremist fringes of our society have turned to bloody terrorism on a few occasions to highlight their existence and publicise their demands (mainly against the US military presence in the Kingdom). Corruption may be the most troublesome of our social woes, for it grows in our midst, fuelled by the race towards material wealth versus the forgotten pride to serve God, King and Country.

The Saudi government and society have shown a keen interest in eradicating these social woes. Crime is severely punished as prescribed by Islam. Drug trafficking is punishable by death, and addicts can receive free and anonymous treatment at specialised government centres. Terrorism is abhorred and sternly dealt with, and terrorists are usually caught, tried and executed. Only the issue of corruption remains without truly objective analysis and solutions, and this is the dormant threat to our future.

To effectively fight these ills, we must not only identify them, but we must also fully comprehend their causes. It is clear that Islam has helped us in our daily lives and in this incredible voyage of development and affluence. The rapid change that has overwhelmed our lives has made some of us forget our Maker, his rules, and his regulations. The race towards wealth, the frustration in not reaching it, the boredom of certain non-productive existences, the influence of false friends, the weakening of the family unit, the few cases of social injustice, these are the real causes for our social woes. There are solutions to them at home, within the school, in the mosque, and in the office. Islam is our cure, but it must be administered with total comprehension to be effective. Islam is not a word or an image, it is the light and essence of the life of the believer and we are a deeply believing society.

If we are to continue to prosper and live in social harmony, then we must help each other without limitations. We must understand the true causes of our ills and find cures for them. We must never let our problems alter the manner in which we deal with each other and foreigners whom we host amongst us. We should never forget our traditions, Islamic values, and the responsibility we have towards the weaker links in our society. A drug addict is a sick human and he must be helped with love and compassion. It is not right to sweep the problem under the carpet hoping that it will go away. The addict will continue to suffer and multiply and as time passes more love will be needed to cure him and those who have become like him. However sick they are, they are our brothers and sisters, and it is our duty to stand by them and help them. The same applies to criminals and terrorists, who must fully endure their respective Islamic punishments, yet at all times be treated with human respect. We must attempt to understand why they have fallen in crime and sin, so that we can eradicate the causes of such mistakes from our lives and avoid further sadness and bloodshed in the future.

How should we treat this sickness called corruption? As Islam prescribes, or in a *laissez-faire* manner? At present, the Kingdom still has enough money for all, and we can hide this small but growing problem if we wish. But is this the right attitude to adopt? Can a government employee forget his national duty for an ill-gotten fortune? Can a private business-man earn contracts by corrupting others? It is important to remember that God owns all wealth and that we must all account for our earnings on the day of judgement. It is clear that cases of corruption in Saudi Arabia are the work of a few weak souls in government and the private sector influenced by foreigners and cronies who gain from our national demise.

Although corruption is much worse in many other coun-tries, it is a growing phenomenon in our society, and this has led to concentrated attention in the international media. It is time for us to take responsibility and stand behind our King in fighting this sickness that is growing and eating at our very soul. It is time for us to truly comprehend what behaviour constitutes corruption under Islamic doctrine. It is time for us to say no to all those who want to use their positions to cheat and blackmail and to expose them to their just Islamic punishment. It is time for us to eradicate corruption from our lives through real accountability and transparency, so that our children can lead an existence where government work is an honour, and serving our King and Country is the privilege that it is.

18

The Charitable Nation

SAUDI Arabia is truly a blessed country that has so much to its advantage. Its population has achieved prosperity and affluence because of the oil wealth, protected by a strong Islamic faith and wise visionary management. We have not had to work as hard as the Japanese or the South Koreans to enrich our economy and build our infrastructure. Our path has been easier than many others, but it has certainly not been devoid of difficulties and obstacles. We have had to fight wars, unravel unfriendly plots, educate an entire nation, and build at the same time. This has been our blessed road, and may it continue in the future.

With so many advantages, Saudi Arabia has distinguished itself over the past 25 years as by far the most charitable country per capita in the world. There are so many projects all over Asia and Africa that have been donated by the Kingdom and which have really changed people's lives in a positive manner. The government has implemented an international aid programme which has disbursed for charitable projects and causes over $60 billion (6 per cent of Saudi GNP) in the last quarter of a century. This is in addition to official aid to

nations through international institutions such as the World
Bank. The generosity of Saudi Arabia far exceeds that of all
industrialised countries whose aid packages are usually
attached to exports or other restrictions while Saudi aid is
mostly in the form of direct grants. This aid programme is
based on the Islamic precept of help for the poor and needy,
but it has also brought Saudi Arabia enormous international
recognition, prestige and political influence.

An indirect form of charity made by Saudi Arabia is the
huge investment (tens of billions of US dollars over the last 50
years) in the holy cities of Makkah and Madina, to enable
millions of Muslim pilgrims to visit the holy shrines for Haj
and Umra. The extent of the benevolence of such a gesture
cannot be fathomed by outsiders, but to Muslims these
investments have opened the path to a multitude who would
never have been able to perform this religious duty. These
huge investments have drastically reduced the cost and ease
of these religious rites, with no charge being required from
anyone for the usage of airports, highways, Haj accommodation, security procedures, medical assistance, etc., contrary to
normal practices in similar cases in all other countries in the
world. A private donor even went to the extreme of air-
conditioning about 16 square kilometres of open space in
Arafat (outside Makkah) through chilled water vapours that
are sprayed into the air, to alleviate the discomfort of the
millions of pilgrims from the extreme heat.

The most interesting phenomenon has been the high level
of private global charity made by Saudis over the past three
decades. This is based on the Zakat, which is a rate of 2.5 per
cent of one's income which must be given to charitable causes
annually. As commercial entities have had to donate this
religious due to the government in Saudi Arabia, private
donations for Zakat and Sadaga (voluntary charity) have gone
to build thousands of mosques, schools, medical clinics, and
orphanages around the world, in addition to the hundreds of

thousands of refugees kept alive by the charity of ordinary Saudis. This desire to help those less fortunate than we are is a genuine human gesture that is not solely influenced by tax or other worldly considerations. It is a need to please God and to satisfy Islamic commandments. It is a reflection of our wish to have our sins absolved and our place in heaven confirmed.

The Saudi people's charitable character is a worthy example for the entire World. It is pure in intention and execution, and it has really made a difference for many unfortunate and destitute human beings. It has attempted to fight the incredible results of war and sickness and balance the charitable shortfalls of others. It is a banner for exemplary Islamic behaviour which advocates peace, love, and charity as the basis for human relations. In this the people of Saudi Arabia have succeeded and they have not let their wealth divert them from their human responsibilities.

The charitable character of Saudi Arabia as a nation has been outstanding, but it has unfortunately not eradicated world poverty and suffering. There are more than 10,000,000 orphans in the Islamic world and a majority of refugees in our planet are Muslims. Only a minority of these receive adequate medical and human care with a shortfall in positive inputs to balance their sad lives. Saudi Arabia cannot hope to solve the problems of the world, but it is necessary that we continue to show the world that we are a good people who always treat others with generosity and compassion, and that millions of human beings of all races breathe easier because we exist.

It is hoped that other nations, especially those in the rich industrialised world, will truly follow the pure example of Saudi Arabia and extend an unconditional helping hand to the hundreds of millions of needy people in our planet. Other religions must co-operate with Islam to remove any and all obstacles to ensure that we can together eradicate misery and epidemics without any political or social restrictions.

These are neither mere slogans nor a utopian dream, but a global necessity in which Saudi Arabia has truly proven itself to be a leader, and where many other countries have unfortunately not been sincere or effective in their actions.

19

The Balance Sheet

THE past pages have described certain important aspects of the state of Saudi Arabia politically, economically, and socially. These show a country on the move, developing in all aspects of its existence. It is a review that identifies enormous advances in infrastructure, industry, human resources, and the standard of living of the entire population. It demonstrates a deeply religious nation in spirit and in deed, with positive effects on its social fabric and national harmony. Saudi Arabia is politically stable, with an efficient system of government that has been able to deliver real results in a most benevolent manner. It is a government that has succeeded in surmounting serious obstacles effectively and corrected mistakes whenever they occurred. It is a system that works and that has every opportunity to prosper in the future.

Saudi Arabia is in a healthy shape, but this does not mean that everything is perfect. There are problems that exist, may they be serious, of small significance, or just lurking beneath the surface of actuality. They are the threats of tomorrow and they must be solved if the nation is to continue to advance and prosper. Solutions are certainly not beyond the reach of the government and people of the country, but they can only be applied if the problems themselves are identified and understood. Solutions to present and future weaknesses will only succeed if the political and social will is firm and unwavering in actual application. No problem is ever insurmountable, and the ills of Saudi Arabia are minute compared to the sheer magnitude of its advantages. The challenge is in the acceptance of the nation of all the facts, and its will for further prosperity and perfection. Saudi Arabia has its past as a blueprint for what it can achieve in the future, but the tools for a bright twenty-first century are already available if we wish to use them.

The future will depend on our ability as a nation to protect the value of the things that have contributed in making us what we are. How far we adhere to the Islamic principles that have kept our social fabric together so efficiently through incredible development has a direct effect on our ability to prosper further. We must protect Islam from the mishandling of men who may attempt to abuse it or modify its applications in a manner that may expose us all to social disaster. They are truly threatening our soul and existence and they must not be allowed to even approach success. Our religious role in the Islamic world, because of Makkah and Madinah as well as our way of life and affluence, is of such importance that our example is crucial for many others. We must not fail other Muslims and our own children.

Oil as the essential source of world energy is crucial for our future growth and affluence. We are dangerously losing ground compared to other oil suppliers and alternative sources of energy, when our reserves are the largest and our production cost is the lowest. How fast we address this huge problem has a direct effect on our economy and the value of our vast oil reserves. It is logical to presume that other sources of energy will arise, and some may be cheaper and environmentally cleaner than oil. It is also logical to believe that these cheaper modes of energy will supersede the importance of oil, in the same manner that oil superseded the supremacy of coal early this century. This would drastically reduce the value of our petroleum reserves that are estimated to last us between 150 and 200 years at our present rate of production (8 million barrels per day). Although we need the cash now to repay our debts from the Gulf War, we cannot raise our production because of the OPEC quotas. Raising production would also cause the prices to weaken, further adding to our dilemma. This is a difficult problem but its solution is crucial to our future as a nation.

The stability of Al-Saud has a direct effect on the health and prosperity of the entire country and its population. As the creators of modern-day Saudi Arabia, through their vision, hard work, and wise decisions, Al-Saud's future is directly linked to the future of the nation. How they govern and how they prosper is synonymous with the performance of Saudi Arabia. This is why the bonds linking the nation together must be preserved and strengthened, and implementation improved by all, so that benefits are truly maximised.

Where Saudi Arabia will go in 10 or 20 years is also dependent on many outside issues that will arise in the future. If we are strong and ready, then we will have a better chance of surmounting the difficulties and benefiting from the advantages. We must never leave today's work for tomorrow as the latter may be shorter than we expect. We should strive now so that our children can enjoy at their leisure the fruits of our success and theirs. It is with this thought in mind that we can continue with our journey of discovery by looking at what Saudi Arabia can become in the future.

Part Three

What Can We Be?

20

The Examples to Follow

SAUDI Arabia has achieved international status as a leading developing nation thanks to the oil wealth and its efficient management over the past half a century. The country, strong with successes and privileges, should be poised for further development and affluence, as all the ingredients that have marked its existence are still very much in place. Yet many questions about the future abound both from Saudis and foreigners. This is a strange situation, because the ills that do afflict our daily lives are very small in comparison to the assets and achievements that dominate our existence.

It is important to address the present fears for the future of Saudi Arabia because they have an effect on the economic, political, and social performance of the population. Uncertainty affects the way we invest and the manner in which we behave. It alters our ambitions and limits the potential of our future. It is certainly caused by our knowledge of our ills, our feeling that they are not fully addressed, and our fears that they will cause us to lose our great affluence. These fears are certainly encouraged by outside interferences that believe they will gain from instability in Saudi Arabia, but the main reason lies in our own hearts and our now complex existence as a nation. We forget how much we have achieved and how we have achieved it. We wonder about the pace of development in the future and the methods to realise it. We therefore feel a paralysis in our existence, as if life stands still for us while it moves swiftly for the rest of the world.

Success is achieved partly through luck, but mostly with hard work. Nations have turned chaos and poverty into wealth and affluence by applying discipline and labour as long-term national targets. They have remodelled their societies through a sincere and patient effort which has made them in a relatively short time examples of global success. Japan and Germany spring to mind and their present affluence tends to make us forget the disastrous condition of these nations in 1945. Other examples of successful societies can be found in Switzerland, Luxembourg, and even Malaysia. They are all diverse societies, with different systems of government and geographical locations, yet they share a national desire for success, the vision of how to achieve it, and the will to implement the difficult steps on the road to that achievement. They are case studies for all developing nations to analyse and emulate and their example should be both copied but also surpassed by simultaneously safeguarding the specific characteristics and strengths of individual societies.

The secret of success lies in people and leadership. It is a balance between civic rights and responsibilities, vision and reality, hard work and perseverance, targets and achievements. Success is the fruit of policies and dedicated implementation in a national and continuous effort. It lies in the understanding by all of the mission which must be realistic and complete. It may entail temporary sacrifice, but the results are well worth the trouble. It is a national quest for education and knowledge, a path of labour and patience, and the road for satisfaction and happiness. Successful nations are not immune from disasters, but they are more capable in surmounting them and in providing a comfortable basic minimum for all in difficult times.

The success of nations in achieving affluence and prosperity for their people should never be confused with mere materialism. Real prosperity is based on more concrete forms of civilised developments that truly affect the standard of living of the population. These include the quality and accessibility of education, the availability of good employment prospects, the harmony within the society, the effectiveness of the justice system, the low rate of criminality, the security of comprehensive social services, the cleanliness of the environment, in addition to the comfort and luxury of material wealth. Once all these ingredients are available in any one nation on a sustainable basis, that nation can realistically consider itself to have achieved success for its people.

Saudi Arabia is a successful country in that it has achieved an enormous amount for its people in a short period of time. Nevertheless, we have not reached the status of Japan, Germany, or Switzerland, although our assets enable us to aspire to such an achievement. We are in a good financial condition, the envy of most nations, but we are still dependent on oil for our foreign currency earnings, and we are heavily indebted following the chronic weakness in oil prices and the costly Gulf War. We will be considered successful when we regain control of the oil markets and we ensure the long-term global importance of that commodity. We must diversify our economy while we have the financial means to do so, in a manner that increases the standard of living of all the population. We must confirm our leadership of Islamic issues by truly behaving as good Muslims at all times because our fellow brethren are looking to us for direction. We must learn to work harder and with more discipline now so that our children can enjoy the best possible future. These should be the goals of our existence and we must realise that we can achieve them if we really want to.

Fourteen centuries ago, our forefathers succeeded in achieving incredible development and prosperity. They started with nothing in their hands but a deep belief in their hearts. They made the World a better place for many people and this lasted for many centuries. Their legacy is very much a part of our present existence. We have so much in our hands now, it is time that we convert it into real and lasting prosperity. To do this, we must believe unquestioningly in our own capabilities and mission, and then we will discover that we are half way down the path to lasting success.

21

The Disasters to Avoid

IN ITS quest for further prosperity and success, Saudi Arabia should never forget what it has at present and how easily it can lose its assets. It is wrong to say that there is so much it cannot go away. Other nations have been in a similar position to Saudi Arabia and today their populations live in suffering and poverty. God gives in abundance, but he also takes from those who do not respect what they have. It is clear that it takes years to build and seconds to destroy. The line between success and misery is thin, but it is delineated by the known facts of sincerity, knowledge, benevolence, patience and dedication. These are facts that should always be present to achieve a happy destiny and avoid the pitfalls of disaster and failure.

Iran lived in more prosperity than Saudi Arabia less than 20 years ago. It was wealthy, powerful, with an advanced industry and a high-growth economy. It was considered the strongest nation in the Middle East and a promising future power. Yet it suffered from ills that grew unchecked in importance and a leadership that became isolated from the majority of the population. The society became corrupt, and in its quest for modernisation the leadership walked away from its social stabiliser, Islam. Along came a man with so many real arguments and beautiful promises of justice, equality and happiness. The people rose to cheer him and make him their leader. He unfortunately failed in delivering most of what he claimed and he has made the life of his people worse and not better. The rule of Islam that he has applied is not what God has stipulated and it is certainly not the religion that we know. Islam is against terrorism, corruption and injustice. The clothing of the leaders does not mean that they are Islamic and it does not allow them to murder, steal, and threaten their neighbours. The Shah may have needed replacing in the eyes of many of his people, but the Khomeini regime has proven to be a disappointment, and the Iranians can only pray for their own salvation and the resurrection of their nation from the claws of possible future misery.

Iraq is a nation that has been blessed with enormous oil reserves and a plentiful water supply. It has been known in the Middle East for its affluent middle class and its highly trained technocrats. Iraq had prosperity and a bright future in its grasp. Along came the Baath political party with its socialist dogma for Arab unity. Dictatorship ensued, only to worsen once Saddam Hussein took control. An era of wars, killings, and international isolation has pushed the Iraqi people into pure misery and the country on the verge of collapse. This is a case study of waste and mismanagement and it is unfortunately not resolved to this day. If and when Iraq rids itself from the grasp of its bloodthirsty ruler, it will need decades to rebuild its economy and society. The millions of Iraqis who have escaped their country will have to return, mourn their dead, and start from scratch the healing process.

There are many other examples of prosperous countries that went astray due to poor leadership and social fragmentation. Nigeria, perhaps the most promising country in Africa, has achieved the distinction of being the most corrupt nation on earth, a nightmare for any serious businessman, and a tale of crime and misery for its huge population. Algeria, once the pearl of the French Empire, wasted away its oil fortune for nothing significant and is today in the agony of civil war. The list of failing nations is long and each one of them is a lesson in its own right for all those who aspire to greatness but are frustrated by what they consider to be slow growth and political stagnation.

Nations that have failed in providing their people with prosperity and security have usually succumbed to a wide combination of ills that have led to misery and severe social injustice. These ills include the cancers of corruption, extremism, social fragmentation and the collapse of the rule of law. They can afflict any nation in a sudden manner, as they ferment and grow below the surface, until they reach a boiling point that makes them erupt as tragedies of international proportions. It is the strength of the social fabric and the depth of the economic prosperity that protect nations from the dangers of failure. Saudi Arabia must therefore continuously strive to strengthen its social foundations and labour at further developing its economic affluence with the protective and stabilising influence of our religion.

Saudi Arabia is a blessed country. In our path to success we should never forget what has made our present affluence. Every step of the way, we must reinforce our assets and what makes us what we are. In all our future reforms, we must remember that Islam, oil, and Al-Saud have jointly made our dream possible. In strengthening them, we are able to realise our future aspirations without exposing ourselves to the risk of misery like so many other nations that have failed. Money should never alter our beliefs, behaviour, and our general attitude towards life, as we are truly deeper in character than the mere emptiness of material wealth, which in itself is only one of the many marks of prosperity of great societies.

22

The Path to Success

SOME people will ask why Saudi Arabia needs to strive for further prosperity and affluence, when it already has so much. They will encourage us to protect and maintain our achievements rather than think of acquiring more assets. They will explain to us our blessings, and the international balance which prohibits the hoarding of wealth by any one nation. They will enlighten us with their beautiful theories of democracy, and prove to us that this is the path to real prosperity and salvation.

These people are partially right, but also partially wrong. We must maintain our achievements and be able to upgrade them as technology advances. We are blessed and this means that we must protect the causes for our blessing. We have never hoarded wealth even when we had enormous surplus cash, but there is no valid international reason why we cannot become as affluent as Japan or Switzerland, and this should never entail others selling us goods that we cannot really use efficiently. True democracy is wonderful for a society that has the tradition and urge for such a system of government. It is a process that has taken hundreds of years for Western nations to achieve and it is as yet not perfect. It can prove difficult to apply in an Islamic monarchy as Khomeini has demonstrated in Iran. Democracy is a national phenomenon and it could be injected in our system of government if the Saudi population requests it. Our system of government itself was designed to be democratic, as it is theoretically based on Islamic principles of social equality, justice, and respect for human rights. Should we not purify it and strengthen it rather than alter it in a disastrous manner that will hurt and not help? Can we not find our own path, with our own methods and traditions, rather than listen to the knowledgeable outsiders who only care about our oil? God has blessed us so much, but he does wish us to strive for further affluence and to share our prosperity with others before he blesses us even more. Then why should we not stand up and show the world that ours is an example of peace, prosperity, and sincerity, a pure Muslim society in true harmony with all nations?

In order to maintain and upgrade what it already has, Saudi Arabia must act immediately to cure its ills. We must strengthen our position in the oil markets before our weakness becomes irreversible, as oil finances our economic livelihood. We must analyse our entire economy and way of life, take all necessary steps to increase our revenue and overall efficiency, and decrease our expenditure, in order to realise our vast expectations. We must diversify where we can to give balance to our finances and our future prospects. We must study our social characteristics and requirements, and address changes in a sincere and determined manner that is fully compatible with our Muslim religion.

The path for Saudi Arabia lies in securing what we already have and aggressively seeking long-term development. If we stand still, we will get even more frustrated and we will lose most of what we have acquired. The path is not easy, as more prosperity means more envious enemies. Fortunately, more prosperity also means more strength, and this will enable us to surmount all obstacles more effectively than before. Kindness and charity should never be confused with weakness and negligence, and the Saudi people should first address domestic issues and through their resolution solve the problems of others.

Saudi Arabia should set as its goal to surpass the performance of such prosperous nations as Japan, Germany, Switzerland, Malaysia, etc. If this can be achieved over the next 10 or 20 years or even longer is not of primary importance. What is paramount is that we agree as a people and a nation that this lofty goal is achievable if we want it, and if we are sincerely ready to put in place the various tools that successful application will require. Once this is confirmed, and the nation stands as one in its drive towards lasting prosperity to the highest international levels, success in achieving those goals will only be a matter of time.

Oil revenue gives Saudi Arabia a clear advantage in economic development, but only if that revenue is used to fuel an overall economic plan that positively shifts responsibilities and obligations in a viable long-term manner. The path to success should be ambitious yet feasible, for we have all the ingredients to overtake the most prosperous nations on earth, and to build a solid financial cocoon for all the citizens of the Kingdom. This means that we must attempt to multiply our present blessings in order to immunise our society from all possibilities of failure, for it always lurks behind every corner in the future journey of nations.

We have to realise as a nation that there is a reason for our present blessings. In this day and age of wars and famines and the misjudgement of Islam by most of the Developed World, it is time for us to show all the others that Islam stands for prosperity and peace for all people. We must make a positive difference for ourselves and for those who need our help. This is our national mission and it is within our grasp. We must act now while we have the material chance and time to achieve overall and lasting success. We must show God, ourselves, and the entire planet that we are worthy of this blessing.

Part Four

How Can We Be?

23

The Agenda for the Future

IN ITS quest for further prosperity and lasting success, Saudi Arabia must take all appropriate steps to strengthen all existing assets and institutions, as well as modifying certain practices and policies. This should lead to a more potent nation politically, economically, and socially, capable of surmounting future obstacles while providing its population with a heightened standard of living. This process will take many years to implement and must be continuous to achieve its many targets. The world continues to advance and we must ensure that our growth is equivalent if not more, so that our already significant position is not only maintained but also improved over time.

Change in no way means that what we have achieved is bad. On the contrary, our many past successes have given us incredible advantages that enable us to aspire to more affluence and prosperity. We are a great nation, responsible and respected, and we must not be shy in recognising this international importance. Our policies have built for us step by step this prominent position and we must continue on this same path of achievement and success. Our ambitions have to

be encouraged and realised by continuing in what we are
doing while improving our efficiency and overall performance, thereby increasing the standard of living of all the
population of the country. We have the human and material
ingredients for lasting success and we have always demonstrated the vision and patience to use them correctly.

It is no use for us to feel frustrated. We have just surmounted an enormous problem (the Gulf War) and we
should be happy that the cost was only material. We should
now get on with our ambitions and lives, for the future awaits
us. We can build a greater nation by understanding our
blessings and mistakes and by working harder to build our
lasting achievements. Saudi Arabia has been and is, it is now
up to all of us to ensure that it will be even more in the future.
This is a challenge that we must be proud to achieve and we
are truly capable of succeeding in all ways. This is a reality
which we must recognise and cultivate fully, for in present
self-realisation lies future prosperity.

In order to strengthen our assets and gear them towards
increased growth, we must review our oil policy and tune it to
future patterns. Oil is crucial to our existence and we have to
ensure our control over its value and global importance. We
must take a close look at our economy and modify it through
privatisations and reforms to ensure continuous balance. Our
management efficiency can and should be increased as this
has a direct effect on our national prosperity. We must analyse
our social fabric so that we are a happy and united Islamic
nation able to confront future obstacles in a strong manner.
We have to be capable of appreciating our blessings as this
reflects directly on our level of satisfaction. We must understand the bonds between government and people and the
rights and responsibilities of all, so that our national fabric is
continuously based on loyalty and mutual respect. The
benevolence of our leadership must always be reciprocated in
our human relations, for this guarantees harmony and

stability. We must always address our problems and fears, for only then can we alleviate frustration and improve our lives, and this has a direct impact on our country's tomorrow.

We have to realise that the key for the future prosperity of our nation and all of its population lies in education and knowledge. The continued development of our human wealth will enable us to renew the pioneering spirit of Islam, in order to enable the future generations to excel in medicine, science, law, engineering and economics. This is the secret of the success of nations as diverse as Malaysia and Israel, and it is the most intelligent and benevolent gift that we can give to our children. Through their mastery of knowledge, they will have lives of a high standard where the emphasis is on mutual respect and social harmony, within a safe and comfortable environment that they will be proud of.

I see Saudi Arabia as a prosperous and developed nation, a global player of high repute and influence. I see us as a proud and honourable people, pious and knowledgeable, an example of respect and virtue to our fellow Muslims and the world. I see us united behind our King, like the fingers of one hand, a fist that fights for peace, equality, and justice. I see a land of wealth and plenty, a haven for all who share our values and aspirations. I see what we already are in our hearts, and what we dream of continuing to build for ourselves and our children. This great dream of virtuous existence is truly within our reach, so let us get on with the task of realising it, without undue fears and apprehensions. Saudi Arabia has an important role to play on our planet, and we must guarantee the maximisation of all its positive ramifications, to benefit ourselves and all other nations.

24

The Oil Policy

OPEC is weak. The Organisation of Petroleum Export-
ing Countries now represents less than 40 per cent of
the world's oil production. It has already lost two
of its members (Ecuador and Gabon), and more oil production capacity is on-stream every day from countries outside OPEC than from within. Venezuela, a founding member,
has signed contracts to double its oil production by the year
2005, without consulting other members and against prevalent and expected future quotas limiting production. OPEC
has a production ceiling for all members and this is continuously ignored by several members (Iran, Nigeria, Venezuela).
This in turn puts downward pressures on prices, therefore
punishing the producers that respect the production quotas.
Yet prices are high enough to stimulate exploration and
added production from outside the organisation. Present
prices make other forms of energy, such as natural gas,
a viable alternative to oil both economically and environmentally. The Nymex (the New York Mercantile Exchange)
has more influence on oil prices than OPEC itself. Short
cyclical shortages and temporary price rises give false hopes,

and UN sanctioned countries (Iraq) are bound to start full production in the future, further weakening the oil cartel.

Saudi Arabia is a founding member of OPEC. It has always acted in a responsible and mature manner as the largest oil producer, guiding the organization through many crises and challenges towards global power and profits. The Saudis have moderated oil prices to balance the needs of importers and producers, and insert stability in the markets. Now the Saudis are suffering the most from the weakness of OPEC. The country's oil production capacity is nearly 35 per cent above the present production quota of 8,000,000 barrels per day. Saudi Arabia has the lowest production cost (approximately $1 per barrel) in the world, yet it cannot generate enough revenue to pay the debts of the Gulf War, sustain the development drive of the nation, and maintain its vast infrastructure. This has caused a chronic government deficit and a stagnation bordering on recession. The Saudis continue to suffer to protect and preserve OPEC, out of loyalty, and in the hope that a miracle will restore oil prices and global demand to not so distant past glory.

The fundamentals are against such a miracle, as oil is plentiful and new fields are prepared for production around the world. Other countries are not constrained by OPEC as we are. They produce as much oil as they can with the hope that Saudi Arabia will continue to restrain its production and support prices, therefore increasing the profits of others. The present price of oil is much lower than rates 12 years ago, and with inflation considered, lower than rates in 1975. But oil prices enable huge natural gas projects to come on-stream around the World (Qatar, Central Asia, North Africa, West Africa, etc.) at an investment of tens of billions of US dollars, and gigantic research programmes to develop alternative sources of energy to replace polluting and what is perceived to be Arab-controlled oil. The situation is getting worse every day and it will become an irreversible process by the beginning of the next century. Oil will then just continue to weaken, with prices at a fraction of their present rates, demand for oil being replaced by alternative sources of energy, our huge reserves eventually becoming nearly worthless, our unprepared economy in chronic depression, and our children's future in shambles.

Saudi Arabia should not remain silent and accept these developments as a *fait accompli* because we have all the necessary cards in our hands to change the situation to our national advantage. We can maintain the value of our huge oil reserves by ensuring that oil is plentiful, competitively priced in comparison to other alternative sources of energy, and globally important until at least the middle of the next century. This will give us the time to convert our oil revenue into other more valuable assets and prepare our economy for the new golden age of Saudi Arabia.

To regain control over the oil markets and our destiny, we must open the taps and flood the world with the cheapest supplies, thereby eventually increasing demand and real usage for petroleum products, slowing down exploration and investment in new sources of supply, and making research and development for alternative sources of energy neither necessary nor economically viable. This would be a bold policy, equally courageous to the one we applied as a nation in 1973 (the oil embargo), and even more important to our future economic livelihood. Saudi Arabia has no alternative to the application of this new pricing and production policy, and we may be surprised at how much support we will receive when we eventually apply it, as it will not only help us but also the entire world economy.

25

The Price War

IF OIL is plentiful, with more reserves being discovered globally and more supply coming on the market, then there is no doubt that oil prices will continue to weaken. There is also no doubt that such a scenario is detrimental to Saudi Arabia in view of the fact that it relies completely on this commodity for its economic needs, in conjunction with its huge oil reserves and the country's very low cost of production. To continue on the present course is against Saudi interests as it enables other producers to increase their production while we adhere to OPEC quotas, and oil prices are high enough to encourage developments of attractive alternative sources of energy. To counter this dangerous situation to our future without wishful thinking of miracles and the false hopes created by temporary cyclical price rises, would mean that Saudi Arabia and its immediate allies in OPEC must dramatically increase their production, and decrease their prices, in a manner that gradually increases their income and restores their control of the oil markets.

In such a scenario, Saudi Arabia could be producing its maximum capacity of 10,500,000 barrels per day within six months, a new increased total capacity of 16,000,000 barrels per day within three years, and another additional capacity of 4,000,000 barrels per day two years after that, for a total production capacity of 20,000,000 barrels per day within five years. It is estimated that oil prices of $10 to $15 per barrel enable additional oil supplies and alternative sources of energy to be developed. For the new strategy to succeed in its long-term goals, Saudi Arabia must fix most of its large new supplies at an average of $10 per barrel for five years, with 7.5 per cent increases annually for at least five years thereafter. This should be done in the form of fixed price irrevocable oil contracts for 10 years, thereby reassuring the buyers of a continuous and ample supply over a long period of time and discouraging other energy investments elsewhere. Fixed oil price contracts will also guarantee Saudi Arabia and its allies an increasing income even in the case that oil prices go below our posted price in the 10-year period of the contracts. This is a distinct possibility in the beginning of the price war as oil supplies will exceed world demand.

The gradual increase in oil production from 10,500,000 barrels per day to 20,000,000 barrels per day will cost approximately $60 billion, and it can be easily financed by Saudi Aramco based on the additional oil sales. If the prices of the various grades of Saudi crude are fixed at between $9.50 and $10.50 per barrel, then net revenue from oil sales will exceed our present national revenue on a reliable and durable basis, especially if we fix the price of all our production. With countries such as Kuwait and the United Arab Emirates, which are our natural allies because they share very similar economic and political aspirations with Saudi Arabia, and others that will eventually join in, OPEC may look different in the future, but it will represent over 50 per cent of global oil production with world demand for the commodity probably increasing at much faster rates of growth because of the lower prices. Saudi oil production will represent over

25 per cent of the global market by the beginning of the twenty-first century, a rate we can sustain for more than 50 years. Saudi Arabia could then plan the conversion of its oil revenue into other assets that will become the mainstay of our economy after the age of oil, when hydro-carbons will inevitably diminish in importance as the main international source of energy.

The oil-price war strategy will face two main obstacles. The first obstacle that will appear is technical, as arguments as to the damage to the oil fields at a high rate of production are a common present occurrence. They stress that Saudi Arabia will be foolish to increase its production to much higher levels as the oil fields may lose pressure in the future. Surely, with the gigantic size and tight grouping of our oil reserves, the excellent experts we have in the country, and the advanced technology available internationally, we can increase our production without damaging our reserves, and we can certainly improve our recuperation rate which is at present well below the world average. A lot of the fears that exist regarding our intentions to substantially increase our level of production are not technical in reality but more political and economic, and this is the second and more serious obstacle we may face. A few important countries and large international companies do not wish to see Saudi Arabia and OPEC once again controlling the oil markets, especially with lower pricing. This interferes with their own control of markets, their present investment strategies in new oil supplies, and their involvement in the development of alternative sources of energy. It is also bothersome to oil producers with smaller reserves which may be depleted in less than 15 years, as their interest lies in maximising short-term prices, and this is not necessarily good for us in view of the conditions of the oil market at present, which can have disastrous effects on our future if they remain unchecked.

We will be told that our actions threaten the very existence of large fellow Muslim countries and will cause widespread misery around the world. These words are untrue, as more Muslims and humans in general will benefit from our actions than those that will suffer. Furthermore, Saudis must address their own existence and prosperity before they start solving the problems of other people which are often caused by political and economic mismanagement by their own governments, and the greed of certain multi-national companies that know no social or human responsibility.

Lower oil prices and a higher rate of Saudi production will not only be beneficial to the Saudis themselves but also to the world economy. Every country which is a net importer of energy will gain tremendously and this is a clear majority of the planet. Even the US will gain in real growth terms as the cost of energy will diminish dramatically, although Texas and Alaska may go into recession. Africa, Europe, and most of the Far East and Latin American economies will be clear winners, as will all oil producers who are able to drastically increase their production. These gains in world economic growth will be substantial and they can be preserved in the long term. They make Saudi Arabia one of the important sources for world prosperity, and this will increase our international influence by encouraging the reliance and protection of others towards our nation and our people. Our actions will further weaken our enemies and diminish their present capabilities for mischief.

To increase the chances of success and overall efficiency, Saudi Arabia should accelerate international downstream investments so that we have greater access to markets for our oil. We should truly regain sovereign control over the total marketing of our crude oil and related products in a manner never influenced by outsiders. It is important that we achieve these actions concurrently with our increased production, especially if we wish to fix our prices on a long-term basis and comfort the markets on reliable and affordable supplies. As the world considers Saudi Arabia to be synonymous with oil, we should truly apply this on a global basis. There are many markets, especially in Africa, Asia, and Latin America, where Saudi Arabian crude oil is weakly represented. These markets will gain in importance in the future, with expansions in refining and distribution waiting to be implemented, and their governments are keen to establish long-term economic alliances with Saudi companies as this will certainly save money and guarantee the stability of supply. We should also look at further developing industries that rely on oil as a raw material or as a source of energy. Our vast reserves will enable us to compete favourably in such businesses and add value to our oil income. The vastly increased associated gas quantities which are extracted with our oil production should not only sustain a gigantic increase in electric power generation, for both local and international consumption as well as usage in other gas dependent industries in the Kingdom (such as petrochemicals), but we could also export this gas to countries as far away as Turkey or Ethiopia through a regional pipeline network.

In 1986, Saudi Arabia started an oil-price war to counter cheating on quotas by other OPEC producers, and excessive supply by non-OPEC producers. Although this was more a skirmish than a war (it was neither long enough nor was it fully supported), yet it did restore order in the markets for a period of three years. We must make order in the oil markets for a much longer period that ensures a permanent reversal of present market trends, which means that the future price war must be applied in a comprehensive and well-studied strategy that includes real investments in our production capacity and general preparation of our economy to achieve overall and durable success. Full understanding of Saudi oil policy will lead to the firm political will necessary to counter expected opposition from countries and individuals who do not share the long-term goals of Saudi Arabia. It will also enable the excellent Saudi technocrats in our oil sector and economy to better serve the nation and its future to the full extent of their abilities and aspirations.

If any one entity can restore order and stability in the international oil markets and benefit the world economy, then it is certainly Saudi Arabia. This is a policy that we can implement successfully if we are thorough in both preparation and application. The important element is time and this is one commodity that is both scarce and replenishing in the history of nations.

26

The New Day

B Y REGAINING total control of the international oil
markets and lowering prices at more convenient levels
of competitiveness, Saudi Arabia is protecting its long-
term prosperity and national interests while promoting
global economic growth. This is perhaps the most urgent and
crucial step towards the strengthening of the foundations for
our future development. But it is certainly not the only step
that has to be implemented if we are sincere in wanting a
successful and prosperous future for our children beyond
present lethargy and feelings of uncertainty.

The oil-price war will give Saudi Arabia a high national
income for a long period of time. This bold action should
never mean that we can relax and spend. It means that we are
now free to implement the necessary reforms that truly
address the country's present problems. We must increase
government revenue to repay mounting debts and build a
significant financial reserve for the future. We must also

trim our national expenditure and restore efficiency to our economy as the present deficit is both unacceptable and abnormal. It is crucial that we continue to develop our infrastructure by properly maintaining what we already have, maximising its uses, and improving on it. Our achievements are many but we have not reaped all the fruits of what we have already built. Let us look at what we already have, what it is really worth to us, and how we can really make the best use of it, before we go buying something bigger and newer. Let us study how others have successfully achieved their goals and use their methods as a blue-print to enhance our own assets and development programme.

We must also analyse our own existence as a nation and modify all elements that have shown long-term weaknesses. Increased revenue when properly invested can mean more prosperity and affluence, but it can also mean social instability and frustration if it is wasted. We must understand our exact condition as a society and address all our present ills sincerely and comprehensively if we are to make a significant positive difference in our lives. We have to build inner strength in our social fabric so that we are immune to the weaknesses of materialism that permeate modern life. We can grow and prosper, but only if we continue to enjoy our national emotional balance knowing fully that our wealth lies in our knowledge and sanity. It is the depth of our sincerity and determination, our belief in God and what he has given us, our knowledge that blessings must continuously be deserved, our dedicated pursuit of education and learning, these are the elements that will determine the level of our national success and prosperity.

Saudi Arabia can improve economically and socially with minor adjustments to its existing national fabric. These adjustments will not only improve the quality and substance of our daily lives, but they will also strengthen our ability to face internal and external obstacles. Our country need not suffer further financial problems and we must not fear decline any more. We can be strong regionally and internationally if we are united and sincere as a nation and if we honestly embrace the elements that have made our present affluence. Our belief in God, King, and Country is a key to stability and prosperity. It is a belief that should be shared by all, ruler and ruled, in the same benevolent trend already marking our history. Our application of Islam as a society, without modifications and hallucinations, is certainly the path to national salvation. So is our very approach to life and our ambitions for our offspring. A vision has made us and it must continue to sustain us. This is our fate and we are advantaged in that we can influence it through our attitude and productivity as Saudis.

Let us then continue on our journey of discovery by looking at the future Saudi Arabia, a country that has positively surprised and that will surpass its past performance, a land that lives for peace and prosperity, and a people who thrive and give. That is the dream and the goal and we will realise it, as we have realised so much before it. But this realisation can only occur if we are continuously thorough and sovereign in taking all decisions and when the latter are based on the long-term interests of the Kingdom of Saudi Arabia, its entire population, and in harmony with our allies and the world community.

27

The Privatisation Drive

COUNTRIES East and West, developed and developing, rich and poor, are all privatising their economies. In this age of extensive and free international trade, the secret for economic success lies in efficiency and competitiveness. Capitalism has shown that the private sector is able to provide better services at a lower cost than government, due to the impetus of profit and competition which stimulate productivity and efficiency. The World Bank and other international financial institutions have made privatisation their motto and tremendous assistance is provided to countries implementing it, in addition to the vast economic benefits emanating from the policy itself.

Saudi Arabia suffers from a chronic budget deficit and a growing national debt, yet the government owns a highly developed infrastructure network that is worth tens of billions of US dollars and that ideally could be privatised. There has been much talk in the country about privatising Saudia (the national air carrier) and the power generation sector, but no concrete steps have been taken up to the end of 1996. The privatisation drive should be comprehensive and carefully planned, in a manner that will increase efficiency, improve quality, ensure future growth, encourage investment in the national economy, and diminish government expenditure on a long-term basis.

To maximise efficiency, the privatisation drive should guarantee independent and capable management targeted towards honesty, profitability, and strong growth. These are the characteristics that should always regulate employment and accountability in all sectors. They should never be weakened by patronising interference and management should be fully representative of the interests of all share-holders, be they government, private, local, or foreign. Government intervention can only occur in a shareholder role if it exists, as the enforcer of clear and mutually accept-able regulations, as the economic support for growth and development, and as the guarantor of the sovereignty of the nation and its laws. Dedicated and experienced managers already exist in multitudes in Saudi Arabia and extensive privatisation will lead to an explosion of this ready talent that will permeate our economy and improve our lives.

The quality of services will improve, as privatisation means the end to monopolies, a commitment to profitability and competition, and an onus on pleasing customers. Privatised companies will have to survive and thrive in the marketplace with efficiency as the key to success. The improvement of services and overall performance should translate into in-creasing demand, higher revenues, lower costs, and more satisfied customers. It will not only make the economy flourish and improve our lives, it should also assist in attract-ing investments into the country. Privatisation will further enable family-owned businesses to expand by going public in a booming stock market, therefore ensuring their continuity and leadership in their individual sectors. But for these goals to be achieved, the quality of services must improve across the board in both the public and private sectors, and transparency must prevail in the economy. All Saudis have to realise that efficiency is the norm and courtesy is required and beneficial to the whole nation. Experiences such as installing a telephone, crossing customs and immigration, or buying shares should always be pleasant for everyone. This only necessitates detailed planning, careful training, positive intentions, and discipline in application. It is a national professional effort that has to be implemented by everyone. It is an integral part of our Islamic traditions and Arab heritage, for it relies on the generosity and the hospitality for which we have been historically famous.

Saudi Arabia today suffers from variable shortages in the supply of electricity, water, telephones, etc. This shortage is certainly due to diminished investments in infrastructure following the Gulf War and it has affected economic growth. It is important to note that shortages also occur when demand grows beyond normal levels because prices of certain services are kept artificially low through government subsidies. The latter are intended to please the population in a benevolent wish to spread prosperity to all. The result can mean excessive demand, unnecessary waste, and chronic shortages. It is best to let the marketplace decide on supply, demand, and pricing, in a manner more tuned to real costs. This in turn encourages growth based on profitability, efficiency, and true market conditions. Government should provide direct subsidies to certain industries and services that are clearly socially beneficial such as the health sector, or strategically necessary such as water for farming, but then careful monitoring is necessary to maximise the advantages, regulate the opportunity costs, and guarantee equality in distribution. Government must also play a crucial role in directing and encouraging future growth, by supporting operators in the economy with precise intentions, timely approvals, necessary protection, and financial guarantees. This will comfort all participants on the level of commitment and dedication of the government towards privatisation and development.

To successfully privatise the economy and maximise the gains of such a strategy, Saudi Arabia must attract huge private investments. It is said that over $300 billion of private Saudi money is invested outside the Kingdom. This money follows stability, confidence, and good investment opportunities. We must attract some of it back home as well as foreign investment and know-how This can be done by organised privatisation based on acceptable regulations and criteria, and efficient investment vehicles. It means a fluid and transparent stockmarket, friendly terms, and active participation by financial institutions. It means government assurances of an enlarged and level field for all participants and controlled operations that disallow dangerous speculation and unfair actions, without any complications and bureaucracy. The possibilities to invest must be open to all, Saudis and foreigners, within recognised and unchanging parameters that are protective of the system but do not thwart its growth potential. We must guarantee stability at all levels if we are to consistently attract investments into our economy. The investor must be sure that his money is safe, and that the law and the government always protect his interests. Operations and commitments must be performed promptly and as contracted, especially those that are already in place but unfortunately not fully implemented as promised (i.e. late payments and the offset programme). The profitable opportunities must exist and they have to be adequately marketed. The quality of life for foreigners must improve, with an emphasis on basic freedoms that are compatible with Islam, and further links established between foreign residents and Saudi Arabia, either through real estate ownership or more ease of movement within the Kingdom for all foreign residents. In this way, we can build on the belief and the market confidence in Saudi Arabia as an excellent and secure investment haven. The first that must be convinced of this fact are the Saudi investors themselves who are at present investing a majority of their funds outside their country.

Privatising present state-owned businesses does not only mean an influx of revenue that will enable government to repay a large portion of the national debt. It also means that the pressure on long-term government expenditure is relieved dramatically as most subsidies and inefficient money-losing operations are not any more on the public books. This in no way diminishes the role of government and its leadership of the economy as the state is the primary regulator and dynamo for all activities. Privatisation gives government the roles that it has been successful in fulfilling and removes from it those functions that necessitate a purely commercial approach. In this manner, the economy becomes more efficient, the future brighter, and the nation more united and satisfied.

28

The Viable Targets

P RIVATISATION of a country's economy is the free-market solution for efficiency, but it also shows the self-confidence of the government implementing it as it does not equate to a loss of control. The drive to privatise while retaining full government support leads to a stronger economy based on financial viability. It is therefore correct to identify the sectors that can be privatised, how far this privatisation should extend, and what model it should be based on. As others have gone through this experience before us, it is logical that we analyse their methods and results and apply-to ourselves those elements that will benefit us most. It is absolutely not necessary for us to implement policies that have failed elsewhere, regardless of why the proposal is made. Saudi Arabia will only continue to grow and prosper if it is completely sovereign in all its decisions and actions. This has been the case in the twentieth century and we must ensure that it remains so in the next century and beyond.

Some of the largest investments in infrastructure have been made in the cities of Jubail and Yanbu, which were planned to be gigantic industrial dynamos. Sabic, Saudi Aramco and a multitude of industrial groups have located their production plants there. Although successful, Jubail and Yanbu have not reached the potential of much smaller Jebel Ali in Dubai. The reason may be because the Dubai facility is an export processing free zone, without any duties or taxes, and our industrial cities are not. It would be easy to convert both Jubail and Yanbu into tax and duty-free export processing zones and unleash their full potential. They will form the perfect platform to launch our privatisation drive. Foreigners can then fully own their factories and warehouses. Services would then be perceived to be at attractive international prices. Visitors to the zones would enjoy simplified visa procedures. Employment opportunities would multiply for Saudis and new investments could be implemented for the large export markets. Many opportunities could be created to bring some of the Saudi money back home to contribute in a profitable manner in the development of the country. Finally, there would be no more excuses for foreign multi-nationals to execute their obligations fully under the offset programme which is now delayed by over $10 billion.

There are a multitude of companies that are at present owned by the government of Saudi Arabia and which could be easily sold to the public. These include Saudia, the national airline, and its privatisation will not only earn the national treasury a significant income, but it should also lead the airline to higher profitability and improved services, without the present delays and service shortfalls normally associated with state monopolies. Deregulating the entire aviation industry on an open sky basis for all Saudi investors will lead to fair competition, lower pricing, and ultimately a better product for the consumer, as has been demonstrated on many occasions around the world (British Airways, etc.). The government could also privatise power generation leading to more capacity growth, realistic pricing, better use of associated gas which will be plentiful and cheap with our higher oil production, and probably a very profitable export product for the country's future. In the same guise, petrochemical production could be privatised and expanded, enabling Sabic and its sister companies to enhance their already global role. Saudi Aramco's oil refining and distribution facilities in the Kingdom and outside it should also be privatised, leading to a vast expansion of this important sector and improved international marketing for our oil with more Saudi private-sector involvement. Water, telephones, highways, hospitals, schools, universities, jails, regional airports, and other forms of infrastructure, should also be sold partially or in full to the private sector to earn the government the necessary revenue which can repay our high national debt, alleviate future treasury expenditure, and hopefully further improve the quality of services produced in the Kingdom.

The privatisation strategy will truly lead to an industrial, agricultural, and service revolution created by the entire population with the guidance, encouragement, and support of the government. It will revive the Saudi banking system by making it central to the country's development drive and enabling it to compete from a point of strength in the international markets under efficient central bank control and support. It will turn the Saudi stock markets into true conduits for investments in the country by attracting international investors with exciting opportunities, easy procedures, complete transparency for all operations, effective controls, and ample liquidity. Most industrialised nations have already privatised their economies in such a complete manner and developing nations are advancing aggressively with that same strategy. We should not be the last to join this crucial trend because we do not at present fully value its incredible advantages, as we may unnecessarily lose momentum and we are threatening our obligation to continue in the development of our nation, therefore enabling it to participate in global economic leadership. Let us take successful examples from the Americas, Europe, Asia, and Africa, and use them as our role models.

Privatisation can occur as a sale of shares to the public, or on a concessionary basis (BOT), or even as a combination of both. The goal is to solve our present economic difficulties, pave the road for our future development, unleash the talent and creativity of the population, and lead to maximised efficiency and benefits for the entire nation. Privatisation in no way lessens the government's sovereign control of the economy and several methods, such as the golden share which the British government has used when privatising strategic industries, can adequately protect all sovereign national interests. The aim of selling government assets to the public is to raise money, but it should also lead to the long-term improvement and expansion of services.

As government raises cash in the medium term and lowers its expenditure in the longer term, it should realise that its obligations towards the national economic drive are in no way diminished. All savings are in reality a shift from the government books to the account of the private sector, significantly diluted by efficiency and increased profitability. Government must always maintain its primary role in directing investment trends as a national policy and in providing necessary financing and guarantees for all nationally significant projects. This support must be extensive and provided equally to all industries based on the importance of projects to the country, in a manner that ensures active economic growth and commercial viability. This continued government support is necessary for the health and prosperity of the entire economy, and it is very much an obligation that must be fulfilled by the body that at all times controls the oil wealth of the nation.

Government will have to subsidise certain privatised sectors such as healthcare, to ensure that they are universally available, affordable for all Saudis, and of the highest quality. This may be done through new systems such as medical insurance which is subsidised by the authorities. It may be in the form of initial near cost gas prices for the power generation industry to stimulate growth and exports in that sector. What is important is to ensure that services are better than before, and cheaper, with a continued leadership role for government without increasing the national debt. On the contrary, the government must establish a substantial financial reserve and, as we will see, this will represent a cornerstone of our country's future economic policy.

29

The Modified Outlook

WITH more control of the oil markets and a privatised economy, it will be time for the nation to assess other ways to increase national efficiency. We must look at all our assets, analyse our way of life, and surely we will discover ways to improve our economic outlook. There is a limit to what can be privatised. Certain assets such as the incredible developments in and around the holy cities of Makkah and Madinah could not be easily operated by the private sector. National defence and its high-tech military facilities are certainly government responsibilities. Air traffic control, the network of Saudi embassies around the world, the fleet of executive government aircraft, these are surely some of the numerous symbols of government sovereignty. We must have them and it is difficult to make these assets produce an income, much less a profit. Difficult does not mean impossible and this is a further strategy for efficiency that we must identify and implement if we are serious about seeking permanent solutions to all our economic woes. It is good to copy the examples that have succeeded elsewhere, but sometimes it is even better to innovate and refine.

Saudi Arabia has invested tens of billions of US dollars over the last 50 years in improvements to the infrastructure in the holy sites, making access to them possible with ease for millions of pilgrims from all over the Islamic world. This infrastructure includes special airport and seaport terminals, highways, accommodation, electricity, water, telecommunications, security, as well as huge expansions to the two holy mosques, enabling them to accommodate millions of believers at any one time. The King Fahad printing press was established in Madinah to produce millions of high quality holy Korans each year for distribution to all Muslims. These investments are the most beautiful achievement implemented by Al-Saud during their entire reign, and history will glorify them and the Saudi people for it. The operating costs for these services are virtually entirely covered by the government budget with little income to soften their burden on the national economy. It is an honour for us Saudis to serve and help our fellow Muslims, but for how long can we sustain as a nation this financial charity, and is it fair for us to impose it on our children? Prior to the advent of oil in the middle of this century, our ancestors had supported much of their existence from the pilgrimage, which was a major source of trade and the population's window to the world. We should look at it as our very unique source of tourism, and a continuous service to our fellow Muslims, with the strong potential of bringing to the country over ten million pilgrims each year (Haj and Umra).

We must convert this financial burden into a serious source of income for the nation in a way that does not eliminate its charitable character. This can be done through the imposition of a Haj levy that must be paid by all visitors seeking to perform their pilgrimage and Umra, based on the time of year and the length of their visit. Such a levy is fair in that it enables these pilgrims to pay for the use of the facilities that we have built at great expense, and they are entitled to good services for their money. As many of the Muslims around the world have low incomes, this system will limit the number of pilgrims annually, as overcrowding has been a serious problem lately. The overall cost of the pilgrimage need not rise with the imposition of this levy, as we can increase the efficiency of this industry through expanded private-sector involvement in the transport and accommodation of these pilgrims as other nations do for religious and general tourism. Furthermore, a lottery can be established in each Islamic country through the network of Saudi embassies operating there to choose a number of pilgrims who may travel to Makkah with all expenses paid. These must be chosen from the poor who are unable to pay their own way, based on the individual country's Muslim population size and financed by a small percentage of the revenue we make as a nation from the Haj and Umra levies. This system will turn a financial burden into a source of wealth that Saudi Arabia deserves. Islam asks all Muslims to perform the pilgrimage at least once in their life, if they are able to. Let us organise the latter part (affordability of the Haj) in a manner which enables us to sustain permanent good services, gives us a return for the huge investments we have been making, while we truly help those that are too poor to have been able to perform this honourable mission during their life.

The defence of the nation is the responsibility of the government and, as we have seen earlier, there have been and there will probably be many threats to the Kingdom of Saudi Arabia due to the oil wealth and the holy cities. The national defence budget has accounted for a large portion of our expenditure, and the large size of some of the threats (Iran, Iraq, etc.) has meant that our armed forces always suffer from shortages in highly trained manpower. Since the occupation of Kuwait by Iraq, we have had to purchase more high-technology weapons at an enormous cost and foreign troops have also been stationed on Saudi soil. This in turn has been vehemently opposed by the religiously radical and nationalist sections of our society who have used the presence of foreign non-Muslim troops as the platform to attack the regime and its policies. This has led to terrorist bombings of American advisors near Saudi military installations and a horrendous loss of life that has shocked the country.

Why can we not address these problems objectively and find appropriate and permanent solutions that eliminate any controversy? We know that we cannot directly extinguish these foreign threats, however many terrorists we catch and execute. Why do we not create an obligatory military service for all young Saudis, as the Swiss do, to increase the size of our armed forces, enable the population to participate in the defence of the nation, instil badly needed discipline and nationalism to our new generations, and save money that is spent outside the Kingdom on incredibly expensive weapons and foreign troops that we may never use, and which are harmful to our long-term independence? As the presence of friendly non-Muslim foreign troops is so controversial, and yet is necessary for the defence of all member states of the Gulf Co-operation Council from large threats such as Iran and Iraq, why can we not as the GCC itself sign a defence treaty with the United States of America and other Western powers which may include the leasing of a fully equipped and manned aircraft-carrier based in the Arabian Gulf? This will eliminate the direct presence of foreign non-Muslim troops on our soil, with all the connotations and costs that this entails, and it should save us from the excessive purchase of more advanced weapons which we may never require, and which make us dependent on foreign suppliers. We could also sign a defence treaty with friendly Islamic nations such as Egypt, Morocco, Pakistan, and Turkey, whereby they can send troops that will have the honour to participate in the defence of the holy cities of Makkah and Madinah, side by side with their Saudi brethren. All these actions should not only diminish this defence problem and its effects on our society, but they will also contribute to enormous savings in our budget with positive ramifications on our economy. They will furthermore reassure nations around the world on the safety of the supply of oil, which is so crucial to their economies and ours, without having to expose their young men and women to unnecessary dangers. We owe this to them as well as to ourselves. We hope that peace amongst the Arabs and the Israelis will finally prevail, removing the sad cloak of evil intent surrounding the image of the US in the eyes of many Saudis, and eliminating their vehement opposition to the essential alliance between Saudi Arabia and the United States of America.

Other sectors of government activities can also become profitable, even those that appear at first glance to be insignificant, if the will and the intention are firm on the path for universal efficiency in the management of our lives. Embassies can increase their income from visas for the increased number of visitors to the Kingdom (free-zones, increased economic activities, more pilgrims, etc.), and more certification fees. The embassy buildings themselves could be purchased by Saudi companies present internationally and then leased back to the government of Saudi Arabia. Air traffic control equipment could be procured on a leasing basis through Saudi companies using the offset programme's financial and technical advantages. The fleet of executive aircraft operated by various government ministries and agencies could be centralised and tendered for the private sector to operate more efficiently. We should look at all issues, however small they may seem, and we should ensure that they are necessary, efficiently managed, and as profitable as is possible.

We could even look at more significant aspects of our existence as a society, such as the ban on female driving, and find logical solutions to problems, without the extremes of naïve publicity stunts and unfounded religious complexes. Domestic male drivers, the great majority of them foreigners, earn over $2 billion annually and spend hours alone with our families in contradiction with Islamic teachings. How long are we going to allow such waste in our lives by fearing what the Prophet Mohammad, peace be upon him, did not seem to fear himself, especially with his wife Aisha? When will we start showing the trust that our mothers, wives, sisters, and daughters justly deserve? How many more billions of US dollars will it take before we wake up as a society and start behaving as the confident Muslims we should be? This is the choice that we must make in all facets of Saudi life, and it is time that we made it if we are serious about turning our country into a permanent example of success and prosperity based on Saudisation, true Islamic principles, and the infinite vision of the founder of the Kingdom of Saudi Arabia.

30

The New Fiscal Policy

IT IS important that amendments are sought for all fiscal
policies to accommodate the modifications that have
been proposed to the economy of Saudi Arabia. At
present, the country depends extensively on government
actions, as oil is produced by the state and regulations mean
that the government is virtually everything in our daily lives.
The level of oil revenues and amount of government contracts determine the economic activities in the entire nation.
With a streamlined oil policy, the general overhaul of our
economy to limit direct government involvement in commer-
cially viable sectors, and the general drive for efficiency, the
responsibilities of government and population are beginning
to emerge in a new light. For these to become clear, the
clarification of fiscal policies must be made, for this will lead
to the delineation of what we expect as citizens from our
government and what are our exact financial responsibilities.

At present, the only official financial obligation on Saudis is
the 2.5 per cent of income Zakat, which is a religious due paid
by each Muslim annually to the poor. In Saudi Arabia, this is
paid by companies to the government in a manner that

resembles taxation and which lacks the required complete transparency crucial to this religious obligation. It is not clear enough if the monies from the Zakat go to the poor or to finance government expenditure, and such a clarification is religiously a must. It would be healthier to call a tax by its name and leave the task for the distribution of the Zakat to the excellent charity organisations that are registered with the government of Saudi Arabia. In fact, if we really organise matters efficiently, we could lead the Islamic world in organising the Zakat proceeds and their efficient distribution. The combined annual income of all Muslims around the world exceeds $1,500 billion, with the Zakat proceeds due from all Muslims therefore in excess of $37.5 billion annually. Surely, this would be enough to eradicate poverty, hunger, illiteracy, and epidemics in the Islamic world if the process was efficiently implemented. This step would put in place a concrete and infinitely beneficial form of Islamic unity in total harmony with global needs and aspirations. It would furthermore force all Muslims to face their religious obligations honestly in a manner that is unquestionably beneficial to the entire Islamic nation (Umma) and humanity at large.

To ensure that crucial services such as healthcare, education, and social security are always of excellent quality without full reliance on oil revenue necessitates the creation of a new dedicated source of income. This can come in the form of a 10 per cent Value Added Tax on all goods and services sold in the Kingdom of Saudi Arabia (with the exception of the free-zones and exports). The income of the VAT can be injected into a government fund specially created to subsidise the now privatised schools, hospitals, and jails, while providing social security payments to the unemployed, whereby Saudis continue to receive comprehensive social services of the highest international standards. The latter is crucial, because you cannot tax people and not give them their money's worth in necessary services, and a say in how their money is being spent, especially in view of the increased income of government. The VAT will perhaps have positive effects in lowering our huge consumption as a society, as this is a crucial aspect of our future economic success. Its income will also help eradicate any and all poverty in our rich nation and address the needs of the destitute and the handicapped, in close co-operation with the excellent specialised charities operating in the Kingdom at present.

Foreigners should also receive free social services of the highest quality, but this should not be directly financed by Saudi citizens. A social security tax should be imposed on the salaries of all foreigners working in the Kingdom, perhaps 20 per cent, with a minimum level salary imposed throughout the economy. All regular residents paying this tax can thus expect good education and healthcare for themselves and their families in a manner that ensures their comfort and security. This will furthermore increase the salaries of foreigners and narrow the gap with the now higher Saudi salaries, thereby hopefully increasing the chances of Saudi employment in the private sector.

The government will further earn annual fees from the privatised industries, such as a share of tolls from highway concessions, landing rights at BOT airports, and profits from gas sales to power generation plants and the petrochemical industry. This is in addition to the present revenue from customs duties which should increase with added economic activities in the country, and higher duty rates on products of countries that impose unfair duties and taxes on our exports (including the hydrocarbon tax on oil). This will diminish our consumption of their specific products, as there are always other alternatives and people should have the freedom of choice. This will also teach those nations that do not trade with us fairly a costly lesson about the freedom of international trade and the important role of our country in it. An official property tax should perhaps be imposed on all real-estate in Saudi Arabia, to limit overt land speculation and create an income stream that will finance municipal budgets, water conservation, and support environmental protection projects that will gain in importance with our increased industrial development and our heightened standard of living.

These new tax modifications should be imposed gradually so that people can plan for them, limiting any social or economic pressures that they may cause. Planning and clarification should cover economic decisions that have to be totally communicated to the population, as it directly concerns their lives and necessitates the support of all. Imposition must be transparent, fair, and efficient, in a manner that eliminates corruption and theft. Certain applied government regulations must be modified simultaneously to mirror all economic reforms in a manner that eliminates unnecessary bureaucracy and waste, as these are frustrations of our present existence as Saudis. Government must guarantee the highest standards and the promptness of payments in all cases, as this is crucial to the credibility and success of the nation and the confidence of all in government policies. We must continue to plan our administration and other aspects of our lives as true Muslims, with honesty and dedication. This is the only path to the permanent satisfaction and happiness of all the people of the Kingdom of Saudi Arabia.

31

The Financial Order

WITH the restoration of oil-market control through a price-war strategy, the privatisation drive, and the revised tax regime, the resulting combined government revenue will exceed present levels by over 50 per cent. Government will also have a lower burden of annual expenditure as the private sector will manage many presently inefficient industries under state operation. This in turn will increase by a great portion the budget surplus, thereby ending the deficit cycle and its repayment issues, and enable the Kingdom of Saudi Arabia to create a national reserve for investments in the future of the nation.

We should learn from the experiences of others when contemplating our country's future. Kuwait built a reserve fund for its future generations with mixed results. It is true that the Kuwaiti reserve was primary in enabling the financing of a significant portion of the cost of liberating the country, yet their experience has been marked by some cases of foreign government interference and financial mismanagement. This will usually occur if huge and successful investment transactions are implemented in an atmosphere of secrecy without the necessary controls and transparency. International business requires discretion, but this can be present in conjunction with firm management practices and accountability. We must also realise that the creation of a financial reserve does not necessarily make it an equivalent to portfolio management as the Kuwaiti model implies. It could take the form of a reserve and development bank, if not by name then by characteristics. This is how Dubai and Malaysia have achieved their present prosperity and how they support their plans for the future. In this model, the government uses its financial assets within an independent corporate structure to support development in the country through the private sector, based on national targets and clear commercial viability. Government support occurs through planning a development strategy for the entire national economy, regulations that enhance the successful achievement of all targets, and the provision of financial instruments and policies that adequately fuel such necessary developments. Growth is then based on assets that theoretically support themselves and each other and hopefully will replace oil as the main contributor to the Gross Domestic Product of the nation. The clear advantage of this model over direct portfolio management of international assets is that most benefits remain and fructify in the country itself, while imports of necessary technology and related equipment and services are increased equally to enhanced economic development and rising local demand, thereby appeasing the international economic powers that resent trade deficits on their balance sheets.

The government of Saudi Arabia must start saving money from the increased national income rather than increase spending on an outright basis. If the money saved is deposited in the local banking system through a transparent reserve fund and the banks are instructed to finance the development of the national economy by the private sector, then a tremendous boom will occur, reaching all facets of life in the country. Guidance must be provided by the government as to national development priorities through a guarantee programme that encompasses projects as well as imports and exports. Therefore, if official policy aims at increasing growth in sectors as diverse as power generation and highways, state guarantees can be provided to private investments in such projects. This will enable developments within the goals of government, to meet national demand and expectations, and to create the jobs that our educated youth need so badly. Imports for equipment and services for such officially supported projects could be guaranteed on the basis of multilateral agreements with other nations wishing to increase their trade with us as well as by our own strengthened banking system. The same can apply to exports of products manufactured in Saudi Arabia, to encourage an expansion of the country's industrial base and assist friendly countries that need commercial financing. This can be coupled with real protection of infant local factories through increased custom duties on competing imports as prescribed by the new international trade agreements.

Tremendous growth will occur in our local banking network and the money supply in the country. As reserves grow and are always deposited in Saudi banks, the latter will be financially strengthened. They will be able to support effectively all expanded economic activities in Saudi Arabia at a very low cost of money and finance the business activities of Saudi companies operating abroad. This will make us more competitive and enable us to penetrate new fields of investments that are not interesting under present criteria. The banking boom could be further increased through the implementation of new rules which would allow foreigners complete and free access to Saudi banking services, with the same secrecy guarantees provided by Switzerland. Not only foreigners will deposit their money with us, but Saudi money should also eventually find its way back home, instead of going to finance foreign activities that do not benefit our nation in any manner.

Everybody demands security and complete protection on their financial deposits in addition to competitive rates of return. Saudi Arabia must totally assure the entire world that it is a safe and profitable haven for all types of investments. To do this, attractive regulations must be established, applied and packaged in an efficient, consistent, and transparent manner. The world must know that our rules are firm and eternal, always protecting the interests of investors within clear and fair parameters. We must ensure stability and liquidity at all times, with no bureaucratic interferences and absolutely no corruption. Payments by the government and the private sector have to be on time, without delays, for all creditors, regardless of their powers or level of contacts. Our banking system must be privately operated but under firm parameters of control by a truly independent central bank (SAMA), in a manner that prohibits theft and dangerous speculation. Islamic banking must be structured, regulated, and supported, so that it is able to serve the public in safety, as prescribed by Islamic doctrine and in conjunction with other types of banking.

Within our reforms of the financial system in Saudi Arabia, we have to carefully analyse the national currency, the Riyal. It is fixed on the rate of the US dollar (3.75 Saudi Riyals to 1 US dollar), because our economy relies on oil exports which are internationally remunerated in the US currency. The disadvantage of this policy is that it makes our economy indirectly dependent on the United States beyond the American role of being Saudi Arabia's most important trading partner and ally. Since the US dollar has weakened against most Western currencies over the last 25 years, we have suffered from inflation because our Riyals are devalued pro rata to the US currency. As we buy the majority of our imports in other currencies, we should peg the value of the Saudi Riyal on the value of a basket of currencies that realistically represent the origin of our imports. We must furthermore price our oil exports on the basis of the same basket of currencies as the Saudi Riyal, so that our imports are compatible with our revenue, without exposing us to inflation and the whims of other nations even if they are our closest ally and friend. Saudi Arabia needs a strong friendship and close economic ties with the United States of America, but our friends must always understand that they also need a strong and stable Saudi Arabia and they should therefore not expose our economy to their own weaknesses, especially when perfectly acceptable and easily applied alternatives exist to avoid unnecessary problems. With 25 per cent of the world oil market, it would be time for Saudi Arabia to reaffirm its total independence in a manner that benefits the population and in harmony with the entire world.

32

The Social Responsibilities of Government

WITH the modified economic structure, the clarification of the financial obligations of citizens and residents, it is crucial that we address certain government responsibilities that will directly affect us as a society. We have seen that Saudi Arabia is a successful nation that has been able to provide its people with numerous advantages, which in turn make Saudi life comfortable and secure. We have also seen that our society suffers from certain ills and latent problems which, although minute compared to the many achievements, must nevertheless be addressed and solved. Many of the economic suggestions in earlier chapters contribute to these solutions, but direct actions through effective policies are necessary in other cases. These actions are the responsibility of our government and the results of their implementation could very much influence our future as a nation.

In present Saudi life, we remark that the new generations are much less motivated than is necessary for our future success as a society that wishes to prosper and develop. They have very high expectations and they have been spoiled in having all their wishes met without effort or delay. The plentiful and cheap services, the unlimited luxuries, the welfare educational system, the subsidised existence, these have all contributed to soften our youth. When the human being gets everything material without much effort, he has very little to motivate him and he usually becomes frustrated with his existence. This situation worsens dramatically if the expected cushy job is no more available, if income is diminished, and if the stabilising factors of family values and religion are weakened by materialism. If the individual looks around him and perceives that he cannot improve his existence, his frustration will multiply. He will feel trapped, imagine social and political injustice, reject traditional cures, and he will be pushed towards any escape from what he perceives to be his unhappy existence. This is perhaps a very simplified explanation for the problems of drugs, terrorism, and general extremism, but it is nevertheless accurate.

We must cease to be a purely welfare state. Society must carry the burden of the old and the weak, but a majority of us must work with diligence if the entity is to succeed and find both happiness and satisfaction. Our government, as our guide in daily life, must take actions to limit the frustrations that plague our existence. Educational quality must improve so that our youth have the spirit of effort and competition ingrained in them early. School should not be a mere physical exercise but rather a challenging mental and disciplinary experience. Effort should be rewarded and failure resolved. Our youth should be treated based on their abilities and performance and not because of their parents' bank accounts or contacts. Our universities should emphasise technical specialisations, as religious guidance is to be confined to the home, the mosque, and the elementary school. It is ludicrous that an engineer's degree is dependent on his knowledge of the holy Koran. God blesses and guides us and demands that we live pious existences, but Muslims are also encouraged to strive to advance their nation and this means that we must be at the forefront of science and technology.

In the early days of Islam, our scholars made discoveries that had enormous positive ramifications for mankind. They strived for excellence and let their knowledge roam where man had never been before. Their religion was the anchor of their belief in success and the light that encouraged them to continue further. Islam is in our hearts, in our thoughts, and in our lives, but it is not necessarily part of a university degree, except in the case of specific religious studies. Every Muslim parent must teach his children the facets of our religion in all its truth, without any socially motivated alterations. Our children have to understand that Islam means kindness, respect, and discipline through-out life. They must learn that mosques have always been thriving centres of religious learning and enlightenment, where peace must prevail. Our religion is our strength and the source of our morality and stability, let us not turn it through our human weaknesses into a technical and social liability that it never was. During the early years of Islam, all knowledge, including secular learning, was greatly encour-aged. For example, Muslims during the Abbasid period translated Greek words, thereby enabling scholars to under-stand the Greek Civilisation and its achievements. A revival of this Islamic quest for knowledge is today an urgent necessity.

The government of Saudi Arabia must address the issue of female employment in our economy based on Islamic doctrine. Billions of US dollars have been rightly invested in educating our girls but they have very little opportunities for employment. This leads to frustration and it is certainly an enormous economic waste, especially in view of the millions of foreign workers who permeate our economy. Other Islamic nations have successfully resolved this issue, perhaps because they could never afford to commit such waste. What a magnificent sight it is to watch thousands of ladies, their hair veiled in Muslim humility, assembling computers in a Malaysian factory. Can we not allow our daughters to be like them? An investor is already establishing a jewellery factory in Riyadh that is planning to employ 3,000 Saudi women. His example must be copied by others and the government must give real financial incentives, subsidies, and support to establish a firm national policy on Saudi female employment. We should not educate our ladies if there are no jobs for them as this will only lead to further frustration, the long-term weakening of our family unit, more economic waste, and instability for the future generations.

Saudi Arabia must address the issue of employment for the thousands of graduates who leave our universities every year. In view of the 5,000,000 foreign workers in our economy, the approximately $18 billion that leaves our economy as part of their annual salaries, the present difficulties in finding appropriate work for our youth, the reluctance of the important private sector in employing the more expensive Saudis, and the dislike of some of the latter for certain jobs, it is time to expand the Saudisation drive through more permanent actions. This can include direct government subsidies for the private sector employment and training of Saudis in a manner which makes our youth cost competitive with comparable foreigners. It also means financial and moral encouragement through a comprehensive media campaign and a deep educational drive for specialisations that our economy needs, from the school to the university through to actual training. Saudisation equates to a long-lasting policy that reaches inside the home and that convinces parents to ingrain in their children the values of hard work and excellence. The best must always be rewarded based on their productivity and sacrifice for their nation. Our goal should be to gradually replace foreign labour with Saudis in a manner that effectively eliminates native unemployment in the country.

The role of the religious police (Heyat al-Amr Bil Maarouf Wal Nahi An Al-Munkar) must be analysed so that its effective benefits can be maximised. We have earlier described the importance of the religious police in fighting alcoholism and drug abuse and in upholding the public morals. We have also addressed the popular criticism against certain excesses of the religious police that emanates from the over-zealousness of some of its members and which is usually expressed by urban residents in the Kingdom. The religious police have two important but distinct functions, namely in showing Muslims the right moral path and in helping society prevent crimes. These are crucial functions performed by good Muslims, but they do not seem to integrate well together in practice. The moral guidance function seems to come under the Ministry of Religious Affairs, while crime prevention is the duty of the Ministry of the Interior. It would perhaps be more effective to split the religious police into two parts and integrate each part under the relevant ministry, so that the various functions are implemented in an organised and government-controlled manner that has popular support and clear social/religious benefits.

The government of Saudi Arabia has to ensure that our judicial system is equal for all and completely based on Islamic law (the Sharia). All judges must always be of a high calibre of integrity and knowledge, making their decisions with compassion, fairness, and independence. Islam is a religion that prescribes both justice and forgiveness in a manner that supports social harmony and peace. Our courts must at all times represent this in a manner that maintains peace and security for all Saudis and foreign residents and that adheres totally to the precepts of our religion.

The final and perhaps the most important social responsibility of the government of Saudi Arabia is the fight against corruption. It must be eradicated from our lives as it is alien to

Islam, an enormous source of popular frustration, and the platform for most of the political opposition to the country and its regime. Corruption is the contemporary malaise of the world, and in our case it can be fought through real accountability for all, severe punishments for culprits, fair and equal treatment in society and the economy, effective and transparent controls, improved remuneration packages, the eradication of unnecessary bureaucracy and obsolete regulations, but most crucially an honest and complete understanding by everyone of the problem of corruption itself and its total rejection by our faith. A clear distinction between the criminality of corruption and normal business activities must be established and identified to all Saudis, so that there is no misunderstanding as to what constitutes honesty and what translates into a social cancer that is so threatening to us. This social cancer can be quickly cured, if that is our true wish, but without a solution our very existence and future as a prosperous Islamic nation is at risk.

33

The National Bond

SUCCESSFUL nations that live in affluence, prosperity, and peace are societies that are united around a common purpose and goal. They are an amalgamation of individuals, clans, tribes, and even sometimes different races, who strongly feel that they belong together, sharing a one nation and the same future. Their unity, motivation, and allegiance to that one entity, in both good and bad times, and their desire to thrive together economically and socially, are a perfect platform for their nation's success. What truly determines the achievements of such nations is the leadership that guides them in their unity and determination. The benevolent leadership that gives its people more than it has taken, that shares with them the moments of happiness and sorrow, that upholds the dignity and morality of the population, this is the leadership that will last because it is respected and loved. The leadership that belongs because of belief and action, and that shares mutual allegiance with its people, is the rudder that steers the nation towards happiness and affluence. The secret of ultimate success lies in that very special bond between people amongst themselves and with their leadership, and their knowledge of the simple fact that together they can achieve their most incredible ambitions, for themselves and for their future generations.

Saudi Arabia carries the name of the family that united the Kingdom and rules it. The reign of Al-Saud is based on the laws of Islam which is the religion of all the citizens of the country. The benevolence of the Royal family, their wish to better the life of the population, the wise development of the vast oil resources, and the continuous adherence to Islamic doctrine throughout development, have earned them the loyalty and allegiance of the citizens of the land. We feel that we all gain by being part of this Kingdom, and we love our King in return for the love which he has shown to us, his people. We will continue to cherish our rulers as long as their rule upholds the true spirit of Islam and as long as their benevolent hand is always extended to each and every member of their flock. We can say this with sincerity and pride as it only increases our dignified feeling of belief and belonging.

Islam guides us to love and respect one another. It instructs us to hold kind relations with our neighbours and to always show generosity to the needy. It upholds the family unit and structures our actions socially from before our birth to after our death in clear definitions of fairness and justice. Islam clarifies the relations between the people and their rulers, based on the fear of displeasing God, allegiance towards the nation and its rulers, benevolence towards others, honesty and truth in all actions, and mutual respect between all people. Islam prohibits the killing of the innocent and the abuse of the weak. These were the parameters that had always guided the way of the greatest leader of all times, prophet Mohammad, peace be upon him, who ruled with love and is immensely loved and whose legacy built an empire seldom matched. To this day, over one billion human hearts beat to his words, and the actions of his disciples affect the condition of the entire planet. The actions of Muslims must at all times adhere to the precepts of our religion and the teachings of our prophet without modification or addition, as this is key to our moral and spiritual salvation. We as Saudis have to lead in this, as our Muslim brethren look to us for guidance and positive example in these troubled times of materialism, extremism, and social deviancy.

As our country grows and prospers, our cohesion and unity should logically increase, as we will have even more to share together. The glory of Islam, the affluence and its comforts, the security of achievement, the respect of others, these are the fruits we wish to continuously reap. We should never allow anything or anyone to stand in the path of our national success, by attempting to divide us and divert us from our mission. We should not allow instability through changes that alter our balance and what has made us and will make us the example of good for others. Our advantages are clear to us and our problems should be even clearer. We will not achieve success if we do not solve them in a firm manner which ensures that they will disappear. We will never be rewarded if we are disunited as a people and a nation.

One should never underestimate the cancers of corruption and extremism as they unravel the bonds that unite the nation. They are problems of fatal importance, by expanding and reproducing beyond control and dividing the ruler from his people. They alter the social balance that anchors the nation and its harmony and they lead to immorality, dissatisfaction and strife. They must be checked with honesty and determination, and controls must be established to prevent their re-occurrence and eradicate their causes. The power of the ruler must be safeguarded by his flock to enable him to better protect their interests at all times. The channels of communications between the sovereign and his people must remain open and effective to ensure that benevolence is real and satisfaction mutual.

The Majlis system for easy accessibility of government officials, as applied in Saudi Arabia, does help the ruler understand the feelings and aspirations of the population. But as the nation grows, issues become more diverse and complicated, and lines of communications may sometimes weaken which could lead to lethargy and frustration. The creation of the Majlis Al-Shoura (the consultative council) has been welcomed by the population, as it creates a new avenue of communication, enables the King to receive advice from knowledgeable representatives of the society, and entices the latter to participate indirectly in the formulation of policy. The next step would be to have the members of the Shoura elected directly by the population, therefore enabling them to truly represent the feelings of the majority in an advisory role and in an independent non-partisan manner. The Majlis Al-Shoura must also have clear powers and functions and therefore effectively become one of the sovereign's tools for rule and control. This same method of popular representation in an advisory role can be extended further in municipalities and local government to increase the communication between government and people. The goal is to truly strengthen the monarchy and improve its already excellent links with its citizens. The tribal fabric that formed part of our social harmony has faded with urbanisation and development, and new tools that fully adhere to Islam must be established to maintain our national balance and our performance as rulers and ruled without racial divisions or other human weaknesses that are alien to our religious beliefs.

Love and loyalty are sentiments that must be felt to be reciprocated. No ruler will unite us or benevolently labour for us like the Al-Sauds have repeatedly shown in this century. We must continue to show them our allegiance, and they will in turn solve our problems and protect our future. They will rule us with Islamic wisdom and justice, and they will maintain our dignity and pride as a nation. With the strengthening of the national bonds of unity, the world will feel our increased comfort and stability, and other nations will join us with their investments and support. This will in turn multiply our prosperity, our stability, and our chances for further future achievements. At the end of the day, we will be in our own territory and what will remain for us is what we have built, our feelings about ourselves and for each other, and our total submission to the Almighty. This is in reality the basis for all our aspirations and ambitions as Saudis and all other nations must understand and accept this, as the world will need an even stronger and more stable Saudi Arabia in the future.

34

The Friends and the Foes

ALL nations that have successfully achieved affluence and prosperity for their people gain automatically in international importance. They are usually respected and their advice has value. They are also envied and threatened, because blind jealousy can unfortunately be a human characteristic and certain foreign governments seem to only be capable of being human in their weaknesses. Saudi Arabia sits on a phenomenal fortune which the whole world now needs and it has the two holiest sites in Islam. It must therefore exercise a complicated foreign policy to maintain peace at its borders and within. With our forecast increased economic development, we must contemplate more complex and sometimes confusing foreign relations as they must effectively conserve the nation's peace and at the same time be acceptable to a great majority of Saudis within clear Islamic criteria. We have to start by understanding who are our true friends and who are our foes, and we must deal with them accordingly within firm long-term policies and alliances that preserve our independence, sovereignty, and prosperity.

Saudi Arabia must look at its relations with other nations

based on two main ideals. The first of these is Islam, which includes within it Arabism, which both constitute our faith and our identity. The second ideal is the one based on pure commercial interests which we must never forget in our quest for prosperity and material independence within the global economy. These two ideals sometimes look contradictory with conflicting interests that are difficult to reconcile in our modern world. But by using the incredible flexibility of our Muslim faith in dealing with all races and people, and in exerting patience when their actions are not always conforming to our national interests and our way of thinking, Saudi Arabia has and will be able to prevail internationally in the interest of its people and peace in the world.

Islam lives in the hearts of over one billion human beings in a manner that should logically regulate every facet of their lives because of the very comprehensive spirituality of the religion. Yet Muslims are divided into sects, tribes, political colours, and countries. They disagree together more often than they agree because their leaderships are under the influence of divergent interests, political pressures, and foreign power alliances. Very few Muslim countries are ruled through Islamic law and they therefore do not ease the adherence of their populations to the lives advocated by the holy Koran and the Sunna. Furthermore, these Islamic populations are not united together into one Umma (nation) and they certainly do not ally with each other because they are Muslim. On the contrary, certain Muslim countries try to destabilise others, as Sudan does with Egypt, or Iran with Bahrain. Although Islam demands unity and forbids the killing of the innocent, these last few years have seen the rise of terrorism by extremist Muslims, mainly against other Muslims. This is unfortunately supported by Islamically cloaked countries who wish to overthrow other neighbourly regimes through skewed religious notions and interpretations that are both destructive and alien to real Islamic doctrine.

The solution is certainly not only the word 'democracy' as we are told so often by the West and as the sad examples of Algeria and Nigeria have demonstrated. We must look deeper than mere slogans, because people want solutions to their problems, be they poverty, social injustice, lack of human rights, or corruption in government and society in general. Islam offers these solutions and our religion is more understandable to all of us than the Western notions of democracy which colonialism had anyhow kept away from us for centuries. Islam and democracy are compatible, as Algeria could have shown had the will of its people been respected, but neither should be used to destabilise Muslims by extremism or force. Saudi Arabia has to continue dealing with Muslim countries the way they deal with us. If they are friendly then they are our brethren, worthy of our help, trade, and hospitality. If they show animosity then we must isolate them and counter their alien schemes. At the end of the day, we must treat all Muslims with charity and compassion and distinguish between the populations that are oppressed and governments that have their own selfish agendas. With tools like the Islamic Development Bank we can expand our commitment to the unity of all Muslims, perhaps one day leading to a common Islamic economic market. Everything must have a start, and as we know by now, spiritual unity is not enough if it is not sincere and complete, but political divisions can sometimes be superseded by economic interests. Saudi Arabia must continue to lead Muslims on this constructive path of peace and prosperity and strive to show Islam in its true beauty and tolerance, which is far from the image that weakness and manipulation have given of our religion to the contemporary world.

Although Arabs share the same religion and the same language, they are as divided politically as the Muslim world. This is not the fault of the Arab people because they do not decide their own fate, which is chosen for them by certain selfish leaders and foreign decisions. Colonialism was primary in dividing the Arab world and attempts at unity that followed independence were based on false imported notions of socialism and the rule of the masses without the guidance of God. Israel is both a reality and our excuse for failure, and the personification of the result of our attempt as a united Arab nation. We should stop lying to ourselves, as Arab countries are not ready politically for true unity, although many other basic ingredients make such unity both possible and necessary (same religion, same language, same origins, same future, etc.). Islam may one day achieve this for us, but this is contingent on the belief in our hearts which must overwhelm all foreign interferences that divide us. Saudi Arabia must continue its wise policy of addressing Arab nations depending on their actions and based on common political and economic interests, as its results are more in tune with the times we live in. Arab unity only seems effective within an economic strategy that applies direct pressure on Israel to encourage it to conclude real peace on the basis of 'Land for Peace', and reap enormous economic benefits as one of the many positive results. Peace is essential for all humans but it should not be finalised with Israel unless it covers all issues in a fair manner, including paramount Jerusalem. An unbalanced peace will not last and this can prove to be worse than the present frozen situation. Peace must eliminate common fears and suspicions, but can one achieve this with intransigence, political manoeuvring, lies, racist prejudices and threats? It takes very few hands to wage war and many hands to build peace. The final issue is how to realistically address human aspirations to bring all hearts together for eternal and mutual bliss.

Economically, Saudi Arabia's ally is the industrial world that depends on our oil. It is clear that we are as dependent on these oil sales as they form the basis for our economic prosperity. When Kuwait was invaded by Iraq and we were directly threatened, it was the West that actively stood by us, especially the United States of America. They did this because of the threat to our oil fields which threatened their own economic interests. This in no way diminishes the fact that their youth died in defence of our country, and for the liberation of Kuwait. We must remember this and comfort these nations as to our stability and our commitment to always ensure affordable and plentiful oil supplies, and comprehensive trade, on the most friendly basis. We have to make them understand that we are in some ways different, with a different culture and traditions and sometimes contradictory opinions on important issues (especially Israeli actions). This emanates from character and identity divergences, as well as geopolitical priorities that should not be changed but rather understood and accepted by all. This should in no way affect the way we all feel and the paramount fact that we must accept, respect, and support each other at all times without economic pressures and political interferences that could be destabilising. They will discover in us a truthful and trustworthy partner, stable, sovereign, and independent, whose future is economically intertwined with theirs. This is key to our future prosperity and our commitment to peace and economic growth in the entire planet.

35

The Twenty-first Century and Saudi Arabia

AS WE approach the twenty-first century, it is important to try to understand how our ancestors of the late nineteenth century had viewed the advent of the present century. Their isolation into many weak and divided territories, and their financial poverty, did not allow them the luxury to plan for an important international role of a united and independent nation. They were too busy fending off the difficulties of everyday life and it must have been a true struggle to be able to dream in such a harsh existence. At least one of them had a dream of a united nation (Abdul-Aziz Al-Saud) and his deep belief in the unlimited power of God brought to us today the reality that is Saudi Arabia. It is truly a miracle that we have achieved so much as a nation in less than a century. We now discuss our potential as a leading economic power and question if our children are able to sustain the strains of further hyper-growth. What a difference a hundred years can make in the life of a society, and what will the next century bring to our country?

Saudi Arabia is today a modern Muslim nation. A century ago, our problems were poverty and division. Now we must deal with materialism and extremism. Our present challenges are similar to those of all other contemporary societies that attempt to realise a good standard of living for their people while strengthening the characteristics that form the identity of their nations within a global framework of peace and co-operation. Up to now, Saudi Arabia has been successful in its efforts at true economic growth by developing an infrastructure network which is second to none and by enhancing its human resources through education and training. The oil sector is an international showcase of high technology and wise management. Islam, which is the identity and belief of the nation, has always been the anchor of social stability throughout the history of this young and independent country. Relations between the ruler and his people are based on benevolence, mutual respect, and allegiance to God. The picture is bright, the advantages are enormous, and the future potential is only limited by our own ambitions.

As we have seen, Saudi Arabia has its problems, but they are minute in comparison to the magnitude of our existing assets. They are problems that most modern societies are facing and that result from both rapid economic development and outside political interference. As we have analysed, all these problems have their solutions and sometimes more than one. What is important is to address objectively these issues of weakness in our national fabric, and find at all times a consensus that eliminates the problems and satisfies both the popular requirements and the laws of God. Throughout our history, we have succeeded in achieving this balance and there is no reason why we should not continue to do so.

What will determine the extent of the future success of Saudi Arabia is the will of the government and the population in strengthening the elements that have made us what we are and how aggressively we wish to pursue prosperity. This does determine how far we wish to reform our way of doing things and the extent of the affluence we want to achieve. It is logical that we want the best for our country and security for our children's future. The real issue is how to reach those targets and maximise the possible gains. We have always been criticised for being conservative and for moving slowly on reforms. This has nevertheless given our nation more gains than any of our neighbours and many nations of the world. There have been some exceptional cases when bold decisions had to be made quickly by the leadership against incredible odds. These cases, including the oil embargo of 1973 and the invasion of Kuwait by Iraq, have shown that a conservative leadership is able and willing to take immediate steps to safeguard the interests and independence of the nation with highly successful results.

It is clear that reforms are necessary, but a sincere and respectful national debate must show the various possibilities and analyse them, as we cannot gamble with our assets and the future of the nation. There is a continuous debate within government that has always existed, and it is for the leadership to decide which path is more advantageous for Saudi Arabia. As history clearly shows, the following generations are directly affected by our present decisions and how we implement them. Time will multiply our efficiency and compound our waste. Our actions will be decisive for our stability as a nation and the bonds that unite the ruler and the ruled. This responsibility has always been a heavy burden that we have assumed with great success.

Our task is really easier than it was for our ancestors for we now know our capabilities and our potential. We have to strengthen our belief in God and what he will enable us to achieve if we wish. By looking deep inside ourselves, we will realise what we are and how far we wish to go. We will understand our faults and how best to address them. We will then understand that the creation of jobs for our youth and the restoration of our control of the oil markets, among other items on our wish list, are material steps that are easily attainable if we want. The solution is in the heart and soul of every Saudi, regardless of age, gender, or occupation. When these hearts and souls unite to achieve their aspirations, in total submission to their Creator and his laws, that is when they will all realise their Saudi dream.

Fourteen centuries ago, the prophet Mohammad, peace be upon him, brought a message of love and tolerance that is very much part of our present existence. He gave an example that we are trying to copy in every facet of our lives. We must ensure that this message is never altered by our human weaknesses, for its purity is essential to our balance and satisfaction as individuals and as a society. In every step we make, in every breath we take, we must remember his words and ways. This will enlighten our vision and provide us with the confidence that will make the twenty-first century a mere threshold for Saudi Arabia on the path leading to salvation and eternal bliss.

EPILOGUE

WRITING this book while simultaneously managing my growing business has been a complex exercise of time allocation, on airplanes and in hotel rooms, over a one-year period. As only very few people knew of my endeavour, my yearning to be alone to write has affected my social calendar and my relations with others. This has been a minor inconvenience in comparison to the happiness that the task of writing has provided me. While researching the material and writing, I opened my eyes and cleared my mind in order to absorb more of what I was seeing and hearing. I encountered many Saudis from all walks of life, be they princes, technocrats, doctors, housewives, etc. I have had the joy of discovering a pool of talent and ambition that I had never suspected could exist. These Saudis were clear experts in their fields and they mesmerised me with their knowledge and their deep belief in God. This has been the single most important result of my research, an encounter with a generation that can lead Saudi Arabia's economic and social revival well into the next century. These young men and women are the living proof that we have achieved a lot in this century and that we will do incredibly well in the future.

I have discovered that our ills could easily be solved if we take a firm decision to do so. It is amazing that our problems are not deeper in view of the magnitude of the change that has occurred within our economy and society. It is very much thanks to Islam that we are a stable society, aware of its obligations and proud of its heritage. The solution to such problems as crime, corruption, and terrorism lies in the true application of the doctrine of our religion without extremism or alterations. It is sad that human weakness has given our religion such a bad image around the world. This is not the reality of Islam, which is the faith of love, freedom, equality, and tolerance. We must through our own daily actions demonstrate the beauty of our faith and defeat this travesty which the weak among us are accepting to commit.

Many Saudis are frustrated and therein lies our main handicap. We are afraid to lose what we have achieved and we feel that other nations are advancing more than us. We know that we have problems, as the international press keeps repeating to us, and we feel that no durable remedies are available or applied. These feelings are natural in any society. They represent the symptoms of the malaise and not the sickness itself. When you start giving the medicine, which in this case means solving the actual problems, the frustration will disappear as if by magic.

We must realise the contribution that our leadership has made to our present existence. Al-Saud have not only united the Kingdom, which carries their name, but they have developed the country in a superb manner and always within Islamic principles. They will succeed in applying the necessary solutions to our national ills as they have so often in the past. Their strength will be multiplied by our own love and support for our King, the Imam of our future.

The world will discover a confident nation living in harmony with itself and others. We will be the cause for enormous economic growth in the planet and many millions of human beings will live better because we exist. Saudi Arabia will always be different and outsiders may continuously misunderstand us. We have to make the effort to communicate with others and to ingrain in them the knowledge that regardless of our differences, we will always be a friendly and reliable partner, respectful of all our engagements, and fully aware of our global responsibilities.

Through our prominent international position, we must continue to protect Muslims everywhere from tyranny and racial prejudice. The events in Bosnia, Afghanistan, Chechnya, and Southern Lebanon must never be allowed to occur again. What a scandal it is to see human beings slaughtered in that very seat of human rights and democracy, Europe, because of their religion. This is the proof that racism and hate are very much alive in this world and that we Muslims are at present a main target.

As I put down my pen and bid you farewell, my last comment on our journey of discovery is that you are going to be very surprised. A star will shine in the near future, and its rays of light will bring warmth and happiness to many parts of the world. Humans will be amazed and they will ask what is the cause of this strange apparition. The answer will come humbly: 'We are the proud people of Saudi Arabia and this is our message of peace and prosperity to the entire planet.'